KINDERGARTEN

Your Child's Big Step

KINDERGARTEN

Your Child's Big Step

BY

MINNIE PERRIN BERSON

Kindergarten Teacher
Ferndale Public Schools, Ferndale, Michigan

Supervising Teacher, College of Education
Wayne State University, Detroit, Michigan

Preface by DR. CLARK E. MOUSTAKAS
The Merrill-Palmer School, Detroit, Michigan

E. P. DUTTON & CO., INC., NEW YORK: 1959

TO

DR. SCOTT W. STREET

who has taught us that the public school of a community must do more than educate its children. It must also elevate the level of enlightenment and weld the expressions of brotherhood among its citizens.

PREFACE

Kindergarten: Your Child's Big Step is a tender, inspiring, and significant account of one teacher's effort to convey to parents and teachers something of the intimate nature of kindergarten life and what it means as the first step in the child's formal education.

The book is written by a person who lives in the day-to-day setting of the kindergarten. It contains not only facts and knowledge of the world of kindergarten, but also the real experiences of a gifted woman whose blend of personal warmth and professional wisdom points to a new way for child and parent, and teacher and parent to meet.

This book is not about kindergarten education but rather is a fascinating presentation of the meaning of the child's first educational venture. It departs from the usual prescriptions and ideas to portray the possibilities of genuine and fundamental relatedness of children, parents, and teachers. Too often the parent is blamed if this first venture is a failure. This is not a book that condemns parents, although Minnie Berson recognizes the impact and influence of the child's home life before he enters school. She values parents and does not dwell on the past or their limitations. She seizes the present moment in her relationship with each parent and struggles to discover ways with the parent in which he may use his own resources in the immediate life with the child, sharing the joys and pains of each new adventure and struggle.

Minnie Berson knows that whether the child's previous experience in the family has been happy or tragic, he brings precious memories to school because every young heart knows how to find what is precious. The five-year-old has not lost touch with the inner strivings of the heart and is still able to realize a living affinity to other human beings and to all growing things.

So the day before the day of kindergarten arrives and images of magic and curious fantasies lie in his heart and in his mind. He comes with wonder and awe, with gladness and rapture. Which of us as parents has not seen this limitless joy suddenly turn to indifference or even violent objection to any idea of school? What happens to destroy the ecstatic joy that exists before the child's entrance? What happens to kill his dream? Here the story is told. He enters a crowded classroom, confined space, inadequate materials, and a restricted environment. The spontaneous joy and enthusiasm soon melt away and he is forced into a conditioning process where he realizes the shocking limitations of an impoverished educational setting.

Minnie Berson helps us as parents and teachers to become aware in a deep and vivid sense what this harsh reality does to the child's limitless curiosity in learning. But she does not stop here. She goes on to show ways in which the child's initial thirst for knowledge and discovery can be sustained.

The curriculum of the kindergarten is explored in such a way that all doubt as to its worth-whileness is dispelled. We see that the kindergarten is certainly a center for guiding development in human relations, but it is also a place where the child engages in self-discovery; in scientific and artistic projects, in the achievement of skills and knowledge that become the basis for further growth and development in the school. Minnie Berson shows how the kindergarten can be a place where the child is free to make choices and explore his own being; to be alone in the center of his being, to play and to work, to let his imagination take him to the limit of his reveries and his dreams.

In this book, Minnie Berson gives each parent an intimate view of the kindergarten and points out how teachers may learn from parents. The child does not leave his home or separate from the parent. The parent maintains, throughout his experience, an active interest in the kindergarten and participates in many significant ways. It is true, in one sense, that the child enters into this new realm of life on his own, but the parent takes a place beside him and participates in his growth by contributing valuable self-resources when they are essential in the development of some school project.

Kindergarten: Your Child's Big Step supports many teachers who are beginning to think for themselves and may spur them on to greater effort. It encourages teachers to open their minds and hearts to the significance of a curriculum which enhances the development of the child's creative individuality.

Though creativity and individuality are recognized and treasured, Minnie Berson does not minimize the significance of knowledge and skills. Perhaps this is the victory the book achieves. It maintains a way to full creative realization of the individual child and at the same time shows how he may learn the facts and skills necessary to healthy human relations and further pursuit of knowledge.

There is a spirit of respect and regard for the parent and the teacher and there is also a firm conviction here that a new and fresh way of life is available to every child who enters kindergarten, a way which does not destroy his initial excitement and joy in learning, but fosters and enhances it. Such a way of life requires that parent and teacher engage in a mutual fellowship and work together toward the child's full realization of potentiality. The beginning is the kindergarten and *Kindergarten: Your Child's Big Step* shows how the child attains social solidarity and growth in individual identity in a setting of living love.

CLARK E. MOUSTAKAS

The Merrill-Palmer School,
Detroit, Michigan.

CONTENTS

KINDERGARTEN

Your Child's Big Step

PRELUDE

Every year, on the first day of school, mothers bring their children to my kindergarten. As the child enters the room, I often see the mother turn her head, to brush away a tear. Or she leaves bravely, only to return cautiously for one more glance, one more assurance that all is well with her child. This is the way I feel now, as Debbie and I walk together in the wonderful August sunset.

Debbie looks at the sky, takes a deep breath of fragrant summer air, and lovingly presses my hand. This is the expression she has chosen to share the beauty of sunset. A glance, a hug, a handclasp have been wonderful ways to communicate in the brief span of our relationship. Yet Debbie, like other five-year-olds, is deeply impressed with words, and uses them with a grace and elegance, precisely hers, to express feelings, reveal thoughts, and ask those wonderful, daring questions about everything and anything.

As we reach the hilltop, we see a man at work on his lawn, his little cocker spaniel at his side. Debbie skips up to them and pets the little animal.

"You like dogs, don't you?" the man asks.

Debbie agrees with a nod and a smile. Then, greatly excited, she announces, "Do you know that next week I am going to kindergarten?"

"That really makes you a big girl," the man answers.

All summer Debbie has been talking and dreaming of kindergarten. Clothes have been bought especially for this occasion. All the members of our household have been involved in these preparations. But Debbie is the most thrilled of all. She can hardly wait to enter kindergarten, to acquire a teacher, to be with a group of children.

Friends have said, as each of my children took this step: "Too bad you can't be his teacher." But I have always answered in the negative. To share your mother with brothers and sisters is wholesome and natural. To share her as a teacher with a room full of children can be devastating. This is Debbie's private experience. She must venture forth to her own teacher and her own group of classmates.

The step into kindergarten is mighty. As a teacher, I cannot recall a single child who approached it casually. Some arrived already rich and thriving; others came troubled, doubtful of their personal worth, and completely captivated by their misery. Yet no child was less than noble on this day of days.

For some children kindergarten is a miraculous year. A weak, unsure child can gain strength and confidence from it. An impetuous child learns the comfort of a steady pace. A timid child may gradually become courageous and free of fear.

But there can also be disaster in this first year of school: a spontaneous child can be squelched; a rare and gifted child crushed, because he's "different" and does not fit. A child reaching out for contact and communication can be frozen into silence and immobility. What makes the difference? A number of factors: the teacher; the situation; and the expectations of the parents, staff, school, and community.

As a kindergarten teacher my concern has been to search for the essence of each child and to share his individuality with those who care most: his parents. Now, for the third time, I find myself in a reversed position. Like all mothers, I wonder how my daughter's teacher will feel. Will she share with me the enchantment that is Debbie? Will the freedom, spontaneity, and joyfulness of Debbie be appreciated? Will there be room also for her independent spirit, or will it be sacrificed for the so-called practical and expedient matters of the situation? I know that what happens to Debbie in this first year of school will be far-reaching.

As Debbie and I continue our stroll, we find ourselves at her school.

Photo by RoseAnna Tendler Worth

"Look, Mommy," she calls. "I can see the kindergarten windows, all nice and shiny. And there is the flagpole. They have taken the flag down, and when I come to school, they will raise it every morning."

All her life a flag has been raised for Debbie. She naturally feels that the school, too, will raise its flag for her arrival. Debbie does not realize that there may be some children in her class who will drain the teacher's energies so completely that she may not be noticed for days at a time. Nor does she consider that others may so charm the teacher that she may never be discovered and cherished as she is at home. She may even become part of the blur of little girls with saddle shoes and ribbons in their hair—unnoticed, unloved, unrecognized during the ten months of the school year, because they lack the traits that demand attention. Even in the kindergarten, affection, acceptance, and recognition can be withheld to a point where a child is humiliated and crushed during this first encounter with school.

Such tragic adversity must be prevented. But it cannot be done by teachers alone. It needs the assistance and support of enlightened, sensitive parents who recognize that just as the boy is father of the man, so the kindergarten is the foundation of education. Communities that offer an excellent kindergarten experience provide an excellent education at all levels.

I have written this book to communicate with parents. This is the goal of many kindergarten teachers who are so busy coping with the pressures and frustrations of crowded classrooms, inadequate buildings, meager equipment and materials, and indifferent communities that they have neither the time nor the energy to acquaint parents with the provocative problems of kindergarten education.

Now let us move step by step with the five-year-old, as he is launched into the exciting, exploring, absorbing world of education through the gateway of the kindergarten.

PART I. INITIATION RITES

> ". . . And ever has it been that love
> knows not its own depth until the hour
> of separation. . . ."
>
> THE PROPHET
>
> Kahlil Gibran

CHAPTER 1

THE KINDERGARTEN SPRING ROUNDUP

A child of five cannot go abruptly from the cozy, intimate life of home to the new, overwhelming experience of school. This tremendous move must come gradually, through a series of carefully planned steps which bring child, teacher, parents, home, and school gradually together in a meaningful association.

For a long time there has been recognition of this need for school-parent meetings at the kindergarten level, but unfortunately some of the systems tried have led to anything but meaningful associations. Many communities, for example, have made an effort to bridge the gap between home and school through a practice called *The Kindergarten Roundup*. Yet, every spring, after participating in this event, mothers and teachers all over the country express dissatisfaction over this meeting. It seems to confuse and frustrate rather than to facilitate the process. The *Roundup* goes something like this:

On a spring morning mothers and five-year-olds arrive at school, eager, radiant, immaculately groomed. Many mothers have walked out on a sink full of dishes, unmade beds, and unfed younger children. They have given hurried instructions to a sitter or have had to depend on a willing neighbor for the care of their little ones, in order to be present at this event.

19

The kindergarten candidate, dressed in his best bib and tucker, is thrilled at the importance and dimension of the occasion. He proudly raises his head, throws back his shoulders, accepts his mother's hand, and falls into step to the rhythm of the roundup promenade. However, the instant they enter the school, mother and child are separated. Children are led to the kindergarten, mothers to the auditorium; or, as one mother expressed it: children in one compound; mothers in another.

Before passing through the door of the meeting room, the mother must show either the child's birth or baptismal certificate as proof of eligibility. Then she is given an assortment of cards: enrollment card, physician card, identification card, and various others, depending on the record-keeping plan of the school.

Finally, when the room is filled, and all the mothers are seated, the principal comes to the platform to say a few words of welcome. Those who know him expect a repetition of former years. Those who have come for the first time are listening for inspiration, eager to have him reveal something of the philosophy and practices of his school. But he has something else in mind. His concern is more with the mother's ability to fill out the cards accurately and completely than with the child's forthcoming education. Thus the principal stands on the platform reading the items one by one, while the mothers, in unison, fill in the blanks—a task that could easily have been done at home.

The teacher is next on the program. She is dressed in a smart spring suit and an attractive blouse. For this occasion her current group of kindergartners have been dismissed. She hopes the new crop and the substitute teacher are not yet engaged in pandemonium. As the teacher stands there, handsome and poised, the mother again looks up at the platform, eager for assurance that her child will be sensitively and lovingly handled. But the kindergarten teacher has other messages to convey. "Be sure," she directs, "to put name tapes on all his wraps. Buy galoshes that will fit in February as well as November. Replace the zippers when they jam. And above all teach him to follow directions."

A mother raises her hand. "Is there any possibility for an individual conference?"

The teacher is matter-of-fact. She expects at least forty children in each session. She will find out next fall whether a child is "well adjusted." If he can't adjust, the home will be notified. Above all, teach him to follow directions this summer, to dress himself, to listen when he is spoken to, and just plain to obey. When you are one of forty, these matters are important.

Now the school nurse comes to the platform. She waits while the mothers of the PTA committee inspect and collect the assorted cards, looking for questions that have been left unanswered. The nurse looks austere in her uniform, and glances anxiously at the door. At last it opens. A sixth grader appears with an armful of Board of Health medical forms. These are distributed, to be filled out by the family pediatrician. Then the nurse makes her recommendations for the summer ahead: a well-balanced diet, plenty of outdoor play, and, above all, a regular, established bedtime.

The mother wonders whether schools realize that parents also know a few facts about the physical and emotional aspects of child rearing. Then she hears that the meeting is over, and coffee will be served in the lobby.

When the mother goes to the kindergarten to claim her child, she learns that he, too, is puzzled and disheartened. He tells her immediately that the most interesting toys were put out of reach. "We couldn't play with blocks. The teacher put the puzzles up high. I asked if they had paint, and she said, 'Next time.' We couldn't play outdoors. Some kids cried for their mothers all morning."

The mother asks gingerly, "Well, dear, what did you do?"

"Oh, we ate Dixie cups and scribbled with our crayons."

"Scribbled?"

"Sure, that's what the little girl next to me said. She said that she can draw but I can only scribble."

Comparisons have started. Already a child feels that his skills are inferior. The substitute teacher was so busy consoling children who cried for their mothers that she had to neglect the rest.

So the *Roundup* ends. For the mother it was a morning of boredom and disappointment; for the child, it was a taste of being part of a massive group with a single baby sitter. This was hardly a worthy initiation into one of life's great adventures—the thrill of beginning one's formal education!

But there are far better systems.

CHAPTER 2

THREE MEANINGFUL ORIENTATION PLANS

Three communities have taken new and decisive steps to pave the way for a meaningful and successful school beginning that involves children and their parents. In Snyder, New York; Ferndale, Michigan; and Liverpool, New York, preparation for kindergarten starts months before the child is officially enrolled in school. All three plans have been conceived and worked out since 1955 by local kindergarten teachers and school administrators. Each community is continually in the process of evaluating, modifying, and refining its program as child and parent participation increases.

Snyder: Preschool Guided Observation Program

During the year prior to kindergarten the four-year-olds of Snyder have the opportunity of meeting under the guidance of a qualified teacher in groups of twenty-five, one morning a week, for a period of ten consecutive weeks. While the pre-kindergarten children have this introduction to school life, their mothers, in a nearby room, are enjoying a similar opportunity under the leadership of an experienced discussion leader.

Before mother and child arrive for their first meeting at school, the home has received a letter of welcome and instruction from the Adult

Education Department, describing the procedure of the first meeting. This gives the mother an opportunity to prepare herself and her child for the occasion.

When they arrive at school for their first meeting, mother and child go directly to the parents' room for registration. Then the mother takes the child to the children's room where a teacher is waiting to greet him and a special hook or locker has been reserved for his wraps and personal possessions. Since the child has already seen the room where his mother will be spending the morning, and has had a cordial welcome from his teacher, he is interested and eager to join his group. If a child is reluctant, however, the mother knows that she is expected to remain with him until he is relaxed and comfortable in this new situation.

Because the regular kindergarten teachers must remain with their groups, there is a special staff for the pre-kindergarten program. It consists of qualified teachers who cannot accept full-time appointments because they have families. But since this program is interesting, and their skills are ideally suited for it, they make an excellent contribution as part-time staff members of the Adult Education Department.

The rooms used for this project are special-activity or multipurpose rooms within the elementary school buildings, used by other community groups such as Scouts, Campfire Girls, and PTA committees. Thus equipment and furniture must be brought out and arranged before the arrival of the children, and stored after they leave. The program of ten mornings, under the supervision of the same teacher, with the same group of classmates, offers the pre-kindergarten child a valuable experience, and definitely prepares him for the year ahead.

In the mothers' group there are equally fine opportunities. The mothers participate in study and discussion groups which include viewing child-development films, reading and reporting to other parents, touring the school, discussing suitability of kindergarten materials, and helping to repair and construct equipment. Mothers observe children and assist the teacher, according to a carefully worked-out plan. Each mother spends one morning as an observer in the kindergarten her child will attend the following year.)High-school seniors, as part of their family-life laboratory work, also observe the children and attend workshops and discussion groups with parents.

How does a father fit into this plan? He comes to school with his child, for a scheduled evening meeting, while his wife stays at home. Father, too, has an opportunity to observe his child in a group, and to participate in discussions with other fathers under the leadership of an educator. Thus both parents are in tune for the year ahead, while the child, in his pre-kindergarten year, has already had a fine taste of life at school.

According to Mary B. Parke, specialist in parent education, and co-ordinator of the program, "The chief aims of the guided observation program are to help parents establish the best possible relations with their children in the early years, and to offer parents the benefits of the many kinds of help available to them from teachers, child specialists, and workers in the field of parent education. It is hoped that by reaching parents and children in these first all-important years, many later problems within the family and between home, school, or community may be successfully avoided."[1]

In a questionnaire designed to evaluate this program, parents expressed the following prevailing views: (1) Children were helped greatly to overcome the fear of leaving mother. (2) Children liked being part of a group, going to school, and participating in the program. (3) Mothers discovered from the experience that their peculiar child-rearing problems were common to other parents, and felt that the contact with other mothers and specialists proved helpful. (4) Mothers suggested more discussion, shorter observation periods, and an opportunity for a progress report of their children.

The staff also offered suggestions. Teachers expressed a need for a larger budget for more and better kindergarten equipment, and an interest in rearranging the rooms. And they agreed with the parents that time should be allocated for a report on the progress of each child. Although this plan was first tried in one elementary school, there are now five groups enrolled in the Preschool Guided Observation Program.

Liverpool: The Kindergarten Workshop and Visitation Program

Many a parent has longingly said, "If I could only see the teacher and talk to her alone, before he starts kindergarten, it would make a great difference!"

Teachers likewise recognize the need for a visit with each child and a talk with his parents before the beginning of school.[2] The teacher knows well that an hour spent privately with each child and family before the kindergartner comes into the group gives her an opportunity to start the school year with a friendly relationship already established between home and school. But how does a teacher find forty, sixty, or more hours to do this job?

In Liverpool, New York, the home-visitation program is now a reality. Mr. Carl Hassel states in the June, 1957, issue of the *School Executive:*

> During the summer, the kindergarten teachers of the Liverpool schools will be employed for two weeks to visit in the homes of the children who will be in their classes this coming year. Their salary for this service is an additional half-month's pay for their yearly contract.
>
> The purpose of these visitations is to familiarize each teacher with the home and allow her to meet and talk with both the parents and child. The *Kindergarten Handbook,* developed by the staff, will be distributed at this time. These visits will be scheduled any time during the summer to suit the teacher's and parents' convenience.[3]

What happens when the teacher comes to the home for a visit? The child meets her as an adult guest, in the warmth and hospitality of his home. At this time he is free to show her his room, toys, pets, and possessions. He may ask questions about the year ahead, and make special plans around his own absorbing interests. "May I bring my turtle to school? Do you know that I like to play with magnets, and I can make them pick up nails and pins? Will Jimmy and I be able to play with those big blocks in the corner like we did that other day, or will we have to let other boys play with us?" There is so much a teacher can learn during this visit!

For the parents, too, this is a great occasion. In the privacy of their home they are free to confide concerns that cannot be brought up in a group meeting with other parents. Some mothers and fathers have known family upheaval, and wonder whether these personal crises have left lasting scars on their child. Others are concerned about their child-rearing practices, and feel they have already made many serious mistakes. "Should I punish him for sucking his thumb?" "Will a reward help him keep his bed dry?" "What do you do when a child goes to bed at a reasonable hour but takes forever to fall asleep?" "Have I been too lenient?" "Have I been too strict?" "Is it normal for my child to eat only the same few things over and over, or should I insist that she taste everything?"

The teacher will not make judgments nor give ready advice. She will offer an attentive ear and an understanding heart. Knowing how a child's parents feel and what they think can only make her work with their child more meaningful. Such complete trust on the part of parents inspires the teacher to share her professional knowledge and insights with them as home and school pool resources for the education and enhancement of the child.

Some families have been blessed with a happy, untroubled life. They, too, want to meet the teacher as a person, to share their good fortune with her, and to feel assured that their child's good life will be deepened and expanded at school. For these reasons, and many more, schools must give parents a private preschool visit with their kindergarten teacher.

Although the home visit is Liverpool's unique pioneering contribution to current kindergarten initiation practices, Liverpool, like Snyder, also offers its parents and children an orientation program of parent workshops and sample kindergarten days.

In Liverpool, instead of employing a special staff for the four-year-olds, the regular kindergarten teachers are freed from classroom duties for three successive Fridays during the spring semester of the school year, to work with pre-kindergarten children in groups of twenty. While children and teacher meet together in the kindergarten, the mothers'

Photo by George D. Margolin

meeting starts with a film, followed by a discussion of such topics as: the purposes and activities of kindergarten, ways of helping the child to a better school start, information on school policies, parent-teacher conferences, health, safety, and other interests and concerns. Questions not covered during the first meeting are put into a box and discussed at the next meeting. These parent discussions are led by elementary school principals, guidance counselors, the district school coordinator, kindergarten teachers, and the community relations director. A PTA committee helps with the serving of refreshments, the organization of car pools, and the distribution of education literature. Mr. Hassel summarizes:

> "On evaluation, our pre-kindergarten workshop and visitation program was shown to produce these benefits to the school and parents: the children (120 participated) will be eager for, or at least unfearful of, school; the parents (also 120) now know most of the answers and will not be telephoning anxious questions next fall; the parents know the school's open-door policy, they will be more ready for parent-teacher conferences and will work more effectively with teachers; and of course the parents now know why kindergarten is a 'must' in the Liverpool schools.
>
> The PTA showed a gain, too, in an eager, friendly body of potential members.
>
> By this early work with the parents, our program has contributed much to a better understanding of the function and processes of the kindergarten program."[3]

This preschool service to the kindergarten child is as vital to the protection of his social, emotional, and intellectual future as are the vaccines that safeguard the health and well-being of his body. To the kindergarten teacher the workshop and visitation plan offers one more way of giving the child a better school beginning. When a community recognizes the teacher's professional worth by providing the time and remuneration for the purpose of laying the foundation of education, the kindergarten teacher cannot help but give the child the fullest measure of her experience, competence, and devotion.

Parents will ask, "If Snyder and Liverpool are taking such careful steps to offer children a good school beginning, what can I do to bring these practices to my community and my children?"

The answer is not a simple one. School betterment occurs only in communities where schools are considered important and teachers are held in high esteem. A community must continually evaluate its education philosophy and practices to prepare its children for today's world.

If Snyder and Liverpool have strengthened education at its initial step, other communities can do likewise by thinking clearly and working cooperatively for the best interests of children.

Ferndale, Michigan: A Year-round Workshop for Kindergarten Parents

A pre-kindergarten orientation program is vital, but it is only the first step. Communication between kindergarten parents and their school should continue throughout the school year for the benefit of the child. Such a year-round workshop is carried on at the Paul L. Best School in Ferndale, Michigan, through a series of monthly meetings between each kindergarten teacher and her parent groups. The series starts the June before the child enters kindergarten and continues until the school year ends the following June.

After the registration procedures, the kindergarten teachers arrange the first evening meeting with mothers and fathers present. This pre-school meeting starts, as do all subsequent parent meetings, shortly after eight o'clock. Teacher and principal both arrive early to welcome parents, especially those mothers and fathers who are new to the school or community.

The principal usually opens the June meeting with a few words of welcome, answers questions about his school and its policies, and then turns the meeting over to the teacher, who briefly presents the goals for the kindergarten year and their implementation. Since this is a young, dynamic suburban community, where parents are deeply interested and well informed on school affairs, parents who have already had other children in school are a valuable resource in helping answer questions of new mothers and fathers. What are the questions that come up at a meeting such as this?

Parents are interested in the teacher's point of view regarding various child behaviors. What are her ways of discipline? What is the daily routine like? Do children have experiences with various art materials? Is the play equipment adequate? Will there be outdoor as well as indoor play? Will the child be helped to learn control, to follow directions, to share, and to take responsibility? Will children have some opportunities for choices and special interests? What are the ground rules to preserve the individuality and personal rights of each child?

The teacher at this meeting indicates that there is a predetermined plan which she follows during the kindergarten year as she works to develop the child's special areas of competence and understanding, as well as his total well-being. She explains also that the kindergarten experience is not aimed at the teaching of factual skills and information, but rather at a cultivation of a child's curiosity, an awakening of his quest for learning, and a growing ability to become a contributing member of the group.[4]

Refreshments for the June meeting are prepared and served by a committee of parents whose children have just completed their kindergarten year. Since many parents are already acquainted, and have worked together on kindergarten and other school projects, the atmosphere is relaxed and friendly. The parents talk of getting together in the summer for picnics, visits, and summer birthday celebrations, and an effort will be made to draw new children and their parents into these activities.

What will the rest of the parent meetings be like for the year ahead? In August, shortly before the opening of school, there will be a work session, where toys will be reconditioned, doll furniture painted, and new hooks for painting aprons installed in the bathroom. While the fathers are working with tools and paintbrushes, mothers will help the teacher arrange the room for the opening day of school by cutting paper, mixing paints, and unpacking books.

In the course of the year the topics for discussion will be determined by the current interests of the group and the events of the children's program. When parents are eager to talk about the physical and emotional well-being of children, the teacher will call upon fathers in the practice of pediatrics, psychiatry, and education to form a discussion panel. One meeting is usually devoted to the school district's facilities for children who need special services, with such participants as the school nurse, speech therapist, school psychologist, and visiting teacher.

When the topics of science, music, literature, and other special areas of learning are considered, parents professionally engaged in these fields as well as speakers from nearby universities are invited to lead these special meetings. The school librarian, a pediatric dentist in the community, an ophthalmologist, and other specialists have been invited to workshop meetings.

The workshop year at Paul L. Best ends with a June smörgåsbord dinner to which each family brings a special dish. Since this community contains families of varied faiths and national backgrounds, there is usually a wide, exotic assortment of foods. The first-grade teachers are guests of honor at this dinner, and the meeting ends with the film, *Skippy and the Three R's,* to set the tone for the year ahead, when the children will have their first formal encounter with academic work.

CHAPTER 3

THE FIRST DAY OF SCHOOL—WHAT CAN GO WRONG?

A good home, loving care, and a child's maturity help him to become ready for school. But there are unforseeable risks and obstacles once the school adventure begins. A child can be overwhelmed when he suddenly finds himself small and insignificant in a tremendous child population. The weeping and homesickness of others can emphasize one's private fear and loneliness and bring forth a surprising tearful outburst. The most obedient of children can be so fascinated by a piece of interesting equipment that he refuses to leave it. Thus the absorption encouraged and praised at home makes him a disrupter of routines and a candidate for discipline at school.

The good intentions of educators who ask the home to prepare a child for the kindergarten experience often interfere with the child's individual ongoing development.

Many parents who have done their job well before the child's arrival at school find that the expectations of the school cause their child needless pain and confusion at times. What good is it to send a child whose individuality has been treasured to a school which cannot begin to continue this practice? Conflicting philosophies and practices between home and school can prove so damaging to a child at the kindergarten level that his school success is threatened.

Photos by RoseAnna Tendler Worth

Patty and Don both came from homes that did their jobs well. Yet neither of these children found the joy and fulfillment that a child should receive in the kindergarten year. A brief look at their experiences will show why.

Patty was charming and alert. Her parents worked as a team of architect and designer, and by the time Patty was ready for kindergarten, she had already enjoyed an exciting and adventurous life as a result of her family travels. When Patty was ready for school, her parents built a home in a middle-class suburb populated largely by professional and business people. From the cultural level of the community the parents assumed that the school would be able to meet the needs of their daughter. Her mother describes Patty's first day at school with regret and disappointment:

It was a beautiful Thursday morning, and Patty was up at six. She talked of school with great anticipation, about her teacher, about the children from the block who would be there, about the new friends she would find. At seven, Patty dressed herself in her new school clothes, eager to make a good impression, and after breakfast, we went together, as the school bulletin instructed us.

The kindergarten room was a disappointment. I was shocked by the sad colors and limited floor space. Not only was this room shamefully small for the number of children it served, but so cluttered with tables and chairs that it was difficult to imagine how a group of children would ever play games there. To accentuate this claustrophobic atmosphere a monstrous slide stood in one corner of the room—an ostentatious, ironical symbol of childhood fun.

The teacher was young, pretty, and obviously a beginner. When Patty and I introduced ourselves, she smiled and immediately ushered Patty to a small table while I joined the mothers sitting in a row of folding chairs at the back of the room.

After the final bell, I counted the children: twenty-eight of them, six to a table, two vacant seats. As I silently surveyed the situation, the mother next to me whispered, "This is really a classroom converted into a kindergarten. Next year, with the new addition, there will be another kindergarten."

The teacher got up and closed the door. She was obviously scared to death of mothers and children alike. The children looked at her with worshipful eagerness. First she addressed the mothers, "We will be here only for an hour today, since too long a first day is not good for children of kindergarten age."

Then she turned to the children, saying, "Boys and girls, I am going to call your names. When you hear your own name, walk over to your mommy, and she will give you a dollar. This will take care of the paper, crayons, and workbooks for the semester."

Soon the alphabetic processional started. Each child, imitating his predecessor, walked, self-consciously, to his mother, held out his palm, took the dollar, and handed it gingerly to the teacher who repeatedly smiled, and murmured, "Thank you, John . . . thank you, Mary . . . thank you . . . thank you."

Before too long a few children became restless. There was a threat of going home from one table, and a great panic when a child's two fifty-cent pieces rolled to the floor with a clang. After the last child walked the child accounting plank, the teacher announced, "Tomorrow say good-by to Mommy at the door, and come in all by yourself."

The mothers were dismissed with, "For the remainder of the week, the children will continue to come for only an hour each morning. We feel that this keeps them from getting restless and gives them a better start. It will work out better for you and your child if he does not coax you into the room."

I was terribly disappointed that this had to be Patty's first day. I felt sorry for the restless children who had been anticipating all summer a morning of play and fun, only to sit in quiet boredom. I felt sorry for the little teacher who was obviously following a plan that had been handed down to her. But Patty, incurable little optimist, said, "I think it will be nicer tomorrow. We won't have to carry money."

What happened during the school year was even more disappointing to Patty's mother than that first day.

The teacher was really a fine young woman, and Patty liked her, but I shall always feel that this was a year of emotional and intellectual retrenchment for Patty. I feel bitter to this day when I realize what my child was ready for, and how little her individual readiness was recognized at school.

As the school year advanced, Patty's mother felt that there was a growing gap between the cherished individuality at home and the expected conformities of school. Her mother describes this experience:

Prior to kindergarten, Patty enjoyed working with many art materials. She painted, finger painted, modeled with clay, used interesting crayon pencils, and made imaginative and delightful pictures. At school, however, it was soon apparent that the emphasis was on the realistic: not only did the teacher draw objects supposedly of interest to kindergarten children, but she expected each child to reproduce a faithful copy of the object she herself had drawn. When the teacher did not use the chalk board, she achieved this result by passing out individual tag board patterns, to be traced, colored, cut, and pasted on pieces of construction paper.

Patty, totally inexperienced and unprepared for this kindergarten hack work, soon became discouraged because of her inability to hold the pattern down with one hand and trace its contour with the other. Her coloring work was constantly out of bounds. Her cutting lacked the exactness required by her teacher. The delightful, spontaneous smearing with paints and scribbling with crayons, so characteristically her own, disappeared, because they were regarded as unacceptable and immature at school. We felt the greatest pain of all when Patty accused us of having been too easy by letting her do *messy work*.

As a professional artist I had done everything in my power to open the art experience to my child. Her teacher, by a total lack of understanding of the freedom and integrity necessary in the creative process, had unconsciously killed this. In the same bold stroke she had also halted my child's expanding individuality by forcing upon Patty self-consciousness and self-doubt.

There were other disturbing aspects of this program. As the school year advanced, more and more efforts were made to introduce academic skills. Practice sheets began to appear daily. There were pages of letters of the alphabet, and rows of numerals. Workbooks came next, and individual pages were sent home filled with red-pencil comments such as, "She needs practice . . . work lacks neatness . . . coloring not on line." These comments were intended as little cues to indicate further home drill on Patty's weaknesses. Patty, as she brought home more and more exercises in printing numbers and letters, kept reiterating the slogan, "This work will help me be a good first grader."

First grader indeed! In all these petty little drills my child's teacher

Photos by RoseAnna Tendler Worth

never found out that our little girl already could read and never went
to bed without a book. Did the teacher know that Patty had lived on
four different continents, that she spoke several languages with friends
of the family, that she had played with children of foreign countries,
eaten their foods, and learned their games?

That overcrowded room had physically restrained my child. The tracing of patterns had cramped the little fingers that so recently knew
freedom and spontaneity. We were especially chagrined and ironically
amused when her last report card was accompanied by a little note
calling our attention to the fact that Patty did not know left from right.

I realized that I was not alone in feeling that my child was having
a most unfulfilling year. Other parents expressed it, too. We had nothing
personal against the teacher but felt that the school itself was in a state
of apathy. I longed for a chat with the teacher, an exchange of view-
points, a swapping of anecdotes, but all I received was a check-list type
of report card with twenty items, and the categories: satisfactory, unsatis-
factory, excellent.

Don was the youngest of four children. He lived in a middle-class
neighborhood close to the campus of a municipal college. Don's mother
had briefly taught kindergarten, prior to marriage, and retained a professional interest in it. She respected Mrs. J., the kindergarten teacher,
for her ability to offer children a creative, stimulating program.

Ten years prior to Don's entrance, the first child in this family started
kindergarten. During the succeeding years, as she enrolled the younger
children, the mother felt that Mrs. J. was developing a growing callous-
ness toward her work. Each year, at the preopening kindergarten tea,
her remarks to mothers stressed more and more the home's responsibility to teach a child conformity. In Don's situation, his mother was
particularly concerned, and made an effort to talk to the teacher, but
in spite of these efforts, Mrs. J. only laughed and said, "If he's anything
like your daughters, it will be a joy to have him."

"He's not at all like the girls," answered Don's mother, but Mrs. J.
was already involved with the question of another mother, and gave no
opportunity to discuss this troubling matter.

On the first day of school Don refused to enter the kindergarten
without his mother. "It won't take him long, perhaps a few days, and

he won't mind being without me," said the mother. But Mrs. J. picked him up, carried him in, and waved his mother away. A few minutes after she returned home, the principal's secretary called to tell her that Don was so upset he had lost his breakfast.

In the office of the principal, Don was crying out his fear and embarrassment. His mother took him home. The next day, when he returned, Mrs. J. said, "He really isn't ready for kindergarten. He's not at all like his sisters."

"If you would only let me stay awhile," the mother pleaded, "we could work it out. He is quite timid in new situations."

"Look," replied Mrs. J., "I have forty-four others in there, and my student teacher doesn't come for another week. I can't cater to Don and his problem."

Don's mother suddenly realized that there had been, through the years, a gradual deterioration in Mrs. J.'s work and morale. This woman had taught for more than twenty-five years, without time off for study or travel. Once this kindergarten had a class of twenty-five children; now there were forty-five.

In her thirties, Mrs. J. was a brilliant kindergarten practitioner. Time, overwork, and lack of incentive had caused her to become hard and ill-tempered. The kindergarten teacher who once treasured the individual child gradually had to abandon him to meet the demands of a massive group. A school constructed for a child population of 800 was trying to house and educate 1,200. What chance did this timid, scared little boy have?

What good is it to prepare a child for a kindergarten that cannot begin to meet his personal and intellectual needs? Homes do not cultivate readiness for school by prescription, but through the sum of: "All the little things that loving parents do automatically—expressing approval and pride in the child's accomplishments, holding him to tasks suitable for his age, singing with him, counting lollipops, pennies, fingers, and toes; providing him with friends to play and squabble with—all these, in the aggregate, are preparation for school."[5]

Criticism of the teacher will not make a better kindergarten. A citizen committee functioning as a study group, working in harmony with the kindergarten staff, is far more constructive. Providing adequate pay, a reasonable class load, inservice training, and a voice in educational policies also help. When a school district dismisses a teacher, principal, or superintendent it seldom attracts a better one to fill the vacancy. In the meantime, the rest of the staff is so threatened that teacher energy is used for job hunting rather than for professional improvement. Teachers all over the country who are dedicated to educating children strive to work in communities such as Garden City, New York; Grosse Pointe, Michigan; Glencoe, Illinois; and Alameda County, California. These communities not only have excellent kindergartens, but top-notch education throughout, because they recognize and respect the professional competence of teachers.

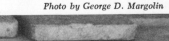

Photo by George D. Margolin

CHAPTER 4

THE CROWDED KINDERGARTEN—
CUSTODIAL CARE REPLACES EDUCATION

What is a reasonable number of children for a kindergarten class? The "Plan of Action," formulated by the Association for Childhood Education International recommends twenty as the maximum number of children to a kindergarten class.[6] Although kindergarten teachers would prefer to maintain this limit, most of them consider twenty-five acceptable, assuming that there will usually be between twenty and twenty-four in attendance.

There are communities all over the country, however, where the kindergarten classes have zoomed to forty, fifty, and fifty-five. Mothers bringing children into these appalling situations tend immediately to express concern and disapproval. Yet when the kindergarten teacher appeals to them for help, the typical reaction is, "Perhaps other children can't take it, but mine is exceptionally well adjusted." Mothers who rationalize in this way may successfully deceive themselves, but they cannot fool the teacher, who knows that an overcrowded kindergarten will affect every child negatively.

What will it do to the teacher? No human being can long continue to carry the burden of two without becoming frustrated, exhausted, and disheartened. When this happens, the quality of the teacher's work falls far below the standards and goals of kindergarten education.

What Overcrowding Means to the Teacher

A teacher from Raleigh, North Carolina, describes the difference in her work as the size of her class rose from twenty-five to forty children:

I know there are not any foolproof recipes for teaching, but if you asked me what it takes to make a good learning situation for young children, I would begin, "Now you take 25 children, a large, wholesome classroom, and a happy, understanding teacher!" Soon you would see a colorful, happy room in which interested children are bubbling with activity. You would see change taking place. You would see learning at its best. The children would all have a sense of belongingness that comes from being part of a group that is not too big. The teacher would have a buoyant spirit because he is not crushed under a load that is too heavy for human shoulders. I know because I have taught 40 children. I have also taught 25 children.

The years that I like to remember were the ones in which I had only 25 children. There was time for all the little things that are important in the child's life. There was time to sit down with each child and help him with individual difficulties. There was even time to find out why some children were having difficulties. There was time to keep anecdotal records for each child. There was even time to sit down at the end of the day and enjoy the sensation that comes from creative teaching.

I like to remember the years that I had only 25 children because we could have a program that was flexible enough to take care of all of the little things that came up in a child's day—something happened in the family; something new was brought into the room; a new discovery was made; a tooth was lost; a new ribbon was worn. These are important things in a child's life and can lead to avenues of learning.

For example, Charles and some of the boys were digging a tunnel during playtime. They began to discover new things in the earth—such as worms, snails, rocks, lumps of coal, bugs. Almost every day for a long time they would bring these things in for a discussion. The digging went on for several weeks and I felt that it was not only an adventure in digging but it was a way to help the boys and girls have a new appreciation of soil and earth and things about us.

When there are only 25 in a group, it is easy to kindle a spark. When there are 40 children in a group, it is easy to snuff a flame! Only a teacher who has taught 40 children can understand the frustration that comes from knowing that you can't ever rekindle the flame that you snuffed today because there wasn't time and the load was too heavy. The real tragedy is written in the lives of those who never really learned to like school, to say nothing of learning to read, or write, or spell.[7]*

As her group grows larger, the teacher finds that children are robbed of her time because a larger group means an increase in mechanical, clerical, and routine duties. Such chores as marking attendance, collecting milk money, distributing bulletins consume a fantastic amount of time. Routines such as dressing, undressing, going to the lavatory or drinking fountain should be casual matters in the course of a morning or afternoon. But when the class is large, these routines have to be carefully organized and carefully supervised to keep the group from disintegrating.

* Reprinted by permission of the Association for Childhood Education International, 1200 Fifteenth Street, Northwest, Washington 5, D. C.

Photo by George D. Margolin

No matter how much she wants to help the individual child, the teacher soon learns that it cannot be done. For the sake of peace, she must ask unreasonable conformity of all her children. Instead of bringing to light the wonders of each child, she finds herself thinking mostly of the group—holding the reins of authority tightly to prevent the aggressive ones from crushing the quieter and more timid children. Thus, she finds herself giving the children less opportunity to think for themselves or to take responsibility for their own actions. As the situation demands more control the teacher begins directing, organizing, and assigning activities, equipment, and materials with increasing rigidity and compulsiveness. The tremendous strain and loss of morale that result from this situation prove so disenchanting to the idealistic teacher that she often resigns to look for a more favorable position.

One school district lost three of its ten kindergarten teachers in a single year. These women were talented, experienced, and highly respected by colleagues and parents alike. As their classroom loads began to rise, they tried to alert school authorities and parents to the negative effects of overcrowding, but no one seemed to care. When their respective groups rose to forty-eight, fifty, and fifty-four children per session, they gave up. Since no qualified teachers could be found to fill these vacancies, the three kindergartens were eventually entrusted to substitutes who lacked even the minimum qualifications for kindergarten work.[8] In this community, as in many others with similar conditions of overcrowding, kindergarten education descended to the level of custodial care.

What Overcrowding Means to the Children

Each child is affected by the emotional atmosphere of his kindergarten. The teacher is extremely influential in creating this atmosphere, but when the class is too large, the overcrowded condition eclipses the teacher's influence.

A study of two kindergarten classes in Salt Lake City, both taught by the same teacher, reveals that the life and learning experiences in the

Photo by George D. Margolin

class of thirty-seven differed markedly from those in the class of twenty-six.

In the bigger kindergarten class there was greater excitement, more noise, and more aggressive behavior. There were frequent acts of pinching, pushing, slapping, and hitting among the children, and some of these behaviors continued on the way home from school. Periods of waiting, especially when children had to stand in lines, proved far more frustrating to the larger group. During conversation periods, there was difficulty with the larger group because there were too many children to listen to, and those who wished to speak had too long to wait. Variations in schedule such as the celebration of a birthday, or a trip to another

Photo by George D. Margolin

part of the building, proved disrupting to the larger group. In the smaller class, however, where the atmosphere was calmer, friendlier, and more stable, the teacher could devote more time to guiding, admonishing, and disciplining individual children. There is no question that the teacher's help to individual children enabled these youngsters to fit more harmoniously into the group.

The relationships established between children also differed decidedly between the two groups. Through the use of sociometric tests, anecdotal records, and other tools for measuring attitudes and behavior, the authors of the study report that:

> The children in the small group helped one another with their leggings and boots. They were kind to the child with cerebral palsy. When she fell or tripped over the wagon, there were no shouts or screams. Such incidents in the larger group were always a signal of tension in shouts, clapping, and sometimes screaming.
>
> The large group had a very immature child as a member. This child needed much help with dressing and other activities. Never once did the teacher note another child assisting her. Several times the members of the larger group refused to go with the little Chinese girl when chosen.
>
> It was noted that the children in the large group appeared to attach themselves to one person; thus they were completely bewildered if this playmate was absent.
>
> The higher quality of cooperative play in the smaller group may be the result of the higher quality of interpersonal relationships in the small group. Or could it be that the satisfying group activity promoted happier sentiments toward one another?[9]*

The contacts between the children and their teacher also differed in the two groups. In the smaller group, the teacher had time to greet each child upon arrival, to inquire about his interests and well-being, and to listen to his questions.

One of the most conspicuous differences between the two groups was revealed in the elaborate, productive, creative work and play activities of the smaller group. The authors state:

* Reprinted by permission of the Association for Childhood Education International, 1200 Fifteenth Street, Northwest, Washington 5, D. C.

It is possible to explain these findings in another way. Namely, the smaller group of children could utilize the space and materials better; therefore, they played more cooperatively. The cooperative play itself permitted more complex and creative endeavors. Out of such satisfying experiences there developed the sentiments of helpfulness toward one another.[9]*

When a teacher from North Carolina writes how it feels to strive for the sensitive, creative teaching with forty children that she once achieved with twenty-five, she is expressing the frustrations of teachers everywhere who are tormented by the same conflicts. A research team studying the effects of life and learning in the two kindergartens of Salt Lake City would report the same findings of two contrasting situations in Chicago, New York, Denver, or any other community. There have been many other studies to show that we cannot compress and pack children in classrooms like sardines in a can and educate them as individuals.[10-18]

Any parent whose child goes to a crowded kindergarten should have misgivings about its effects upon his future school career. But worry is hardly enough. In June, when a school district knows how many prospective kindergartners it can expect, the school board, administration, teachers, and parents should form a study group to help alleviate the situation. If this group does its work well during the months of July and August, the five-year-olds of its community will benefit in September.

* Reprinted by permission of the Association for Childhood Education International, 1200 Fifteenth Street, Northwest, Washington 5, D. C.

CHAPTER 5

WHAT COMMUNITIES CAN DO TO ALLEVIATE
OVERCROWDING IN KINDERGARTENS

Building more classrooms is the obvious solution to overcrowdedness. Although it is hoped that a massive school-construction program will eventually emerge, school districts must continue to find immediate and "temporary" solutions for children who are about to enter school.[19]

What can a parent do to assure his five-year-old a good start when there is no construction program in sight? Very few school buildings have available space to convert to kindergarten use. Communities have tried to provide two teachers instead of one in overcrowded kindergartens, but this plan still leaves double the children in half the space, without giving either teacher a feeling of satisfaction in her teaching.

The only way to reduce the size of a kindergarten class when an extra classroom is not available is to reduce the time a kindergartner spends in school. The two most popular plans for part-time kindergarten attendance are, "The Split Shift Plan" and "The Three-Day-a-Week-Plan." For years communities have used these plans to preserve kindergarten education, and happily discarded them after school construction solved the problem. "We did not like to have our kindergartens on a split shift," says a principal from Oak Park, Michigan, "but it was better than closing them." Now the Oak Park children are back on a full-time schedule again, thanks to a bond issue which made possible the construction of more classrooms.

When a school district reduces the time a child spends in school, it is usually for the child's best interests. In response to this reluctant and desperate action there will always be a vocal minority of parents who refuse to listen to reason. These parents, like other concerned citizens, should have their say. But the plan adopted should be for the welfare of the district's kindergarten children rather than for a handful of noisy, selfish parents who insist that their children attend full time regardless of the consequences.

THE SPLIT-SHIFT PLAN

A school in Oak Park, Michigan, recently was faced with the problem of being able to provide two kindergarten rooms and two teachers for a kindergarten enrollment that called for three teachers and three rooms. An extra teacher was hired, and the children were put on three daily shifts from 9:00 to 11:00, 11:00 to 1:00, and 1:00 to 3:00. The two senior teachers used their own kindergarten rooms. The new teacher had to rotate between the two rooms. Thus Teacher A used Room 1 from 9:00 to 11:00 and from 1:00 to 3:00. Teacher B used Room 2 from 11:00 to 1:00 and 1:00 to 3:00. Teacher C used Room 2 from 9:00 to 11:00 and Room 1 from 11:00 to 1:00.

The teachers did not like this plan, but they recognized that shorter sessions with smaller groups were better than full mornings of overcrowdedness. Eventually, as they worked into the schedule, they added fifteen minutes to each session for the benefit of the children. When teachers in neighboring communities complained about parental indifference, the teachers participating in this program felt that their school district had embarked on a wise course.

Parents found that the split shift conflicted with mealtimes and other household routines, but they were so eager to make the kindergarten plan a success that they hastened to organize car pools and walking groups to help one another. Such cooperation strengthened school and community ties. It also helped pass the bond issue.

THE THREE-DAY-A-WEEK PLAN

This schedule is a modification of the alternate-day plan, which operates by dividing a large kindergarten group in half, with each half attending on alternate days.[20] If alternate-day attendance continued for ten months of the year, a kindergarten child would have one hundred days of school out of a possible two hundred. But parents object to alternate days because there are weeks when a child goes to school only twice. Thus, as a conciliatory measure, the three-day-a-week plan emerged.[21]

The three-day-a-week plan divides a class in two equal groups, like the alternate-day schedule, with Group 1 attending Monday and Friday, Group 2 coming Tuesday and Thursday, and the total class coming on Wednesday. Teachers feel that the day when both groups attend together is full of frustration and pressure, and not profitable to the five-year-old, but they are willing to accept this as a compromise measure.

Overcrowdedness is a hardship which must be faced and controlled if kindergartens are to survive and the kindergarten experience is to open a clear pathway to education. A recognition of the problem and a willingness on the part of school boards, parents, and teachers to arrive at solutions together are the best plan of action until more classrooms can be constructed.

SUMMARY

This section of the book has been concerned with the child's arrival at school: an opportunity for sample kindergarten days during the semester prior to school attendance; workshops for kindergarten parents to acquaint them with the goals of kindergarten; a forerunner parent-teacher-child visit; and a community plan to assure a sound teacher-child ratio. Now we are ready to take the next step, to look into the kindergarten and see how a child of five spends his time at school.

PART II. THE CURRICULUM OF KINDERGARTEN

"In your longing for your giant self lies your goodness:
and that longing is in all of you."

THE PROPHET

Kahlil Gibran

CHAPTER 1

WHAT IS THE KINDERGARTEN CURRICULUM?

The kindergarten curriculum is a design for the education of the five-year-old. It is not a mere course of study where all children must achieve a bare minimum of measurable traits to arrive at a group of itemized goals.[22] Curriculum involves the more subtle and extensive processes of strengthening physical powers, deepening emotions, developing greater social warmth and sensitivity, and elevating intellectual achievement and competence.

When school authorities give prospective kindergarten parents a handsome welcoming brochure (often produced in a public-relations office) which announces that kindergarten is the place to learn sharing, responsibility, work habits, respect for others, enjoyment of books, expression through music, obedience to authority, sportsmanship, self-control, and numerous other values and skills, they oversimplify a complex, lifelong process. These values and behaviors do not grow by prescription. They advance in the kindergarten year through a good life with other children, the guidance of a teacher, and the child's receptivity, which is tremendously influenced by his experience prior to kindergarten. Broadly, like any other curriculum, the one for kindergarten must be designed to cultivate values and refine behavior while it nurtures intellectual depth and skills. How does a teacher do this with brand-new scholars of five?

In assuming the responsibility for the curriculum of a kindergarten class, the teacher has two clear-cut obligations. First, she must stimulate, facilitate, and help each child develop his own curriculum. Second, she must offer the total group a taste of the intellectual and artistic fruits of the culture.

The little child is a born learner. From the very beginning of life he learns through his senses, muscles, body, and every part of his being. When he comes to kindergarten, he is still trying to "find out." He never

Photo by RoseAnna Tendler Worth

takes for granted the wonders that his eyes have seen, his ears have heard, his fingers have touched. He returns to the same objects and places repeatedly, to feel again, look again, listen, and learn again. And out of these endless investigations come questions, hypotheses, deductions, and a maturing of the senses, emotions, and intellect.

The kindergartner wants to know about everything and anything: Why does the white mouse but not the hamster have a tail? Why do you put snails but not salamanders into an aquarium? What is the difference between the toad and the frog? What makes rain? How does water turn to ice? Why are some people brown and others white? Why does a turtle lay eggs on land? What makes a butterfly?

His own firsthand experience and the guidance of an adult are the little child's best intellectual tools. The five-year-old never ceases to pry, seek clues, pursue, and probe everything about him. His research methods are inborn and sound. The kindergarten environment must be designed for the preservation of these qualities. The teacher must continue to feed the intellectual yearnings by her own methods of challenge, stimulation, crystallization. She must walk along the learning path with the child at various points, and sense when the time is ripe to turn him loose on another series of private explorations. She must help him link the learning of the moment with broader knowledge, and become aware of the interlocking and interdependence of all knowledge.

The child scholar, like any other explorer or discoverer, cannot store and hoard his intellectual experiences away from others. He must communicate with his peers by using his sharing, planning, and conversation times to offer his products, ideas, possessions, and abilities for scrutiny as well as recognition.

In kindergarten, the creative process is often crude, sometimes idiosyncratic, but always meaningful to the child. Once initiated, it must be nurtured. Here, for instance, is how it works with Gary.

Gary arrives daily, with assorted pieces of lumber and nails. He is at the carpentry bench every morning, sawing, hammering, sanding, drilling. These activities were contemplated while Gary was still in bed, eyes fixed on the ceiling, thoughts on the work of the morning. Gary

Photo by RoseAnna Tendler Worth

thinks of this work at the carpentry bench with the same excitement that an author thinks of a new chapter. Gary is going to make a boat!

There will never be a boat like this anywhere, because it is Gary's boat, constructed with his special design and ingenuity, of the materials he chose, for the purposes he conceived. Day after day Gary arrives with his materials, making boat after boat, no two alike, each more complex than the previous one. The teacher can crush Gary by interfering with this self-propelled endeavor. She can tell him that he has been at the carpentry bench long enough, and insist that he try something new. This is often done under the pretext of making a child "well rounded."

The other children are saturated with the spirit of Halloween but Gary cannot get involved in these festivities, for the school librarian has found a new book on boats for him. Up to now he thought only of a deck and mast as the essential parts of a boat. This book has pictures of ribs, a pilothouse, bow, stern, hull, galley, mast, rudder, and numerous other parts, each with a special function.

This is an exciting discovery for Gary. The new knowledge is now superficial but gradually it will become integrated, substantial, and part of Gary. The book goes home for a week, says the librarian, and she will find more books on boats to help him with his work.

Now Gary's father is drawn into this pursuit. As they scan the book together, he wonders how this enterprising interest began. And Gary reminds him of the time they sailed with a friend. Now the father is more amazed than ever that an experience at age three should become an absorbing interest at five.

In his study of boats, Gary learns many other things. Wood, for instance, is hard or soft, and it has different names, depending on the tree from which it comes. At first any two pieces could make a satisfactory boat for Gary. Now Gary has more sophisticated ideas of structure. "How long is this?" he asks the teacher, and she brings out a ruler to show him the number of inches. The ruler becomes part of the carpentry equipment, and Gary learns to identify numbers in order to measure his own wood.

The purposes of tools become clearer as Gary's competence in handling them increases. At first he was contented to saw for the sake of cutting, and hammer for the sake of pounding. Now he uses tools with purpose and deliberation. He also becomes acquainted with the brace and bit, the plane, the screw driver, and a variety of nails, tacks, and screws. Shellac is brought in by his teacher so that he may waterproof one of his boats, and he learns that you never clean a shellac brush with water, only with alcohol. A boat painted with opaque water colors and finished with a coat of shellac becomes a work of art in the kindergarten.

This is Gary's personal curriculum. To interrupt or distract him would break off an intense experience in learning and self-direction. This is academic freedom at the kindergarten level, originating with a little boy's eagerness to make a boat. Out of this interest, respected and nurtured by the teacher, grow a variety of skills: an expanding concept of numbers, ability to use a ruler, an enriched vocabulary, a greater knowledge and ability with tools and construction materials, and a firsthand experience with such liquids as shellac, alcohol, paint, and varnish. Gary has also been introduced to books as a way of *finding out*, and now he buttonholes every available adult to read to him about boats.

Gary's activities at the workbench gradually developed from the level of fun and play to the level of learning through problem solving, because of the teacher's involvement and guidance. While Gary prefers to be at the carpentry bench during the work-play periods, Judy is at the chalk board, learning to print her name. John is trying to fit the shapes of a parquetry puzzle into a twelve-inch box. Andy needs help at the abacus. Susan wants to know why the needle inside the little compass starts spinning when she holds a bar magnet over it. All kindergarten children are absorbed in their own special interests. All need respect, guidance, and recognition.

The Curriculum of the Kindergarten Group

Even though the individual child in a kindergarten follows his own special interest for part of each day, he still learns, plays, and works with the group when he is not pursuing this interest. Below is a brief bulletin one kindergarten teacher sends to parents each month. Although she had to omit many details for the sake of brevity, this report gives a broad picture of some of the experiences that take place in one month of kindergarten.

REPORT OF JANUARY

As you probably have heard from your child, we studied birds this month. We concentrated on the following eight winter birds: the red cardinal with his little peaked cap, the woodpecker, blue jay, chickadee, goldfinch, English sparrow, junco, and the nuthatch. We found the nuthatch especially interesting because he has the habit of eating upside down. We brought bread for the birds, popped corn, and added cheerios and apple wedges. We put this food on the fir tree in our play yard, and watched the winter birds at their feast. We also went on a short bird walk in the nearby woods.

This tremendous preoccupation with birds was revealed in the children's paintings and other art work. The colors and forms were totally uninhibited and extremely delightful, but far from realistic.

We learned various poems and songs this month, with the children especially fond of the following group: "The North Wind Doth Blow," "Mr. Woodpecker," "Mr. Owl," "The Crickle Crackle," "The Mitten Song."

Even in the midst of winter we studied about the growing things in the various planting boxes at our school. We also visited a greenhouse and saw some plants growing in vermiculite soil under a fluorescent light. Billy Jones called it an "indoor garden," and it certainly was a lovely sight in January. As a result of this trip, the children should know the coleus, geranium, four-o'clock, snake plant, and the African violet.

A few days after going to the greenhouse, we were inspired to do our own planting by cutting carrots two inches from the top and putting them in little pebbles picked up on our playground. We also rooted sweet potatoes, white potatoes, and onions in water. Now we are counting the days (ten, to be exact) when we should see the first sprouts.

The subject of weather has been of interest to many of the children. Since the atmosphere refused to make the weather we ordered, we went into the school kitchen and manufactured some weather of our own. We heated a kettle till the water began to steam. By holding a cold pan over the steam we made rain. We learned that when the outside temperature was freezing (32 degrees), rain would turn to snow. Naturally, our experiments grew and grew, and when the big snowstorm finally came, some of our children felt directly responsible.

A snow walk around the school grounds brought squeals of delight from the children as they looked at the designs and patterns of snowflakes under a magnifying glass. With the magnifying glass now a full-fledged tool, we hope to introduce the microscope next.

Upon our return to the warmth of the kindergarten room, the children learned how to make snowflakes with paper and scissors. The elements were so inspiring that the teacher improvised at the piano, and the children danced a snowflake dance of their own creation, alternating group and soloists, as inspiration grew more exciting and daring.

Photo by RoseAnna Tendler Worth

The carpentry bench is busy now, and the supply of band-aids is going down as our little boys learn to hit the nail on the head. Along with this enjoyment of muscular and manual labor we have been soothing our souls with lofty music.

At rest time, we have been relaxing to a recording of Grieg's "Piano Concerto." The children are quite familiar with the themes, and as they rest, there are wonderful expressions on their faces when favorite passages emerge.

MARGARET BARTKO*

The above report indicates what can happen in a kindergarten in a month. These children had informal and rudimentary experiences in music, literature, science, art. It is miraculous that in an atmosphere where there is so much play, little children come in contact with so much learning experience and information. It is even more exciting to see how a kindergarten group spends a typical day.

* Andrew Jackson School, Ferndale, Michigan.

CHAPTER 2

THE KINDERGARTEN DAY

Parents often say wistfully, "I would like to know what a day in kindergarten is like. How does the teacher manage to keep the merry-go-round in constant motion?" The kindergarten teacher is most successful in her daily plan when she is most sensitive to the pace and interests of the children.

What does the little child need to spend a worth-while morning or afternoon in kindergarten? He needs in his daily school life a simple sense of peace, sequence, order, and flexibility. The body has its rhythm and need for vigorous physical activities, intake of nutrition, elimination of waste, tranquillity, and repose. The highs and lows that inevitably come and go when one lives and works in a group must be synthesized. The intellect must not only remain full of curiosity and discovery, but become increasingly mature in its ability to organize, analyze, and re-organize knowledge and thought.

The kindergarten teacher needs to be both intuitive and scientific in helping the child spend the day in the most natural and fruitful way. Some experiences she must offer to the total group while others need to come to the child in support of his own special initiative and method. The teacher must have a healthy respect for the peak of child excitement; yet she needs the skill to slow down his pace and help him maintain a healthy equilibrium all through the day. Thus the kindergarten

63

schedule alternates between quiet and active periods, times for the group to work together, and times for the child to explore and pursue his special interests and develop his special skills.

EVENTS OF A KINDERGARTEN DAY

In the typical three-hour kindergarten day the following events usually occur:[23, 24]

> Arrival
> Planning and Telling Time
> Outdoor Play (usually followed by bathroom, a midmorning snack, and a brief rest)
> Group Experiences (lessons involving the total group)
> Work-Play (followed by a brief cleanup)
> Group Experiences
> Dismissal

A child feels a sense of security when he knows how the events of his day will go. This knowledge gives him an opportunity to look forward to the group lessons as well as to plan his own special activities. Yet there must also be enough flexibility in the schedule to allow for the spontaneous and unpredictable events that add such joy to the kindergarten day.

Arrival, Planning, and Telling Time

The kindergarten child usually enters his classroom with great anticipation and excitement. He can hardly wait to take off his wraps, to greet the friends he saw only yesterday, to be welcomed by his teacher, who usually sits among the children. What adult could barricade herself behind a desk when there are such exciting matters to relate?

A baby was born to John's mother last night. Karen has on new shoes, size 12½, and red. Jack will be six tomorrow, and he has a strange feeling that a new two-wheeler will arrive. Judy's mother did not feel well, so Judy served herself a breakfast of dry cereal, juice, and toast. Teddy has been wearing a walking cast, and the doctor removed it with a little saw that buzzed and hummed.

Photo by George D. Margolin

Photo by George D. Margolin

Many children have special plans, and wish to announce them to the group. Jeffrey and Joe are wearing their cowboy boots again because they want to continue playing "ranch." Sam and David have brought Indian feathers, and they want everyone to stay away from the little hill on the playground because it is their lookout point when the cowboys come.

Certain activities are a daily must with some children. Bruce announces that he will ride the tractor. Grace plans another outdoor period on the new tricycle. The same group of little girls will be sitting on top of the jungle gym, playing their game of "birds in a treetop." Jeannie and Mary Ann will pick up twigs to draw pictures on the strip of bare ground near the slide. Mark wants someone to help him haul stones in the red wagon. Susan and Joy plan to fill their wheelbarrows with leaves again.

Some children bring things to show and share. Nancy has a kit with bubble bath, soap, and perfume, for bathing the dolls. Neil came with a special book and some shells from Florida. Steve wants to know if there will be time to walk to his yard and see the new puppies. Joanne has learned a "piece" and wants to play it on the piano. And so it goes, this time for greeting each other on each eventful day.

Outdoor Play (9:00–9:50)

By 9:00 the children are ready to go outdoors. Some of the equipment, such as the merry-go-round, jungle gym, tunnels, sandbox, swing, and slides, is stationary. Movable pieces, such as boards, barrels, sawhorses, teeters, wagons, bikes, wheelbarrows, jeeps, are portable, and the children use them in different combinations on the playground.

Photo by George D. Margolin

Much happens in this approximate hour. Children have an opportunity to run, jump, pull, climb, and dash about to their hearts' content.
A group of "cowboys and Indians" are engaged in dramatic play. Nature's seasonal display of falling leaves, intriguing mud puddles, snow,
ice, sleet, spring buds, ants, birds, grasshoppers offer opportunities for
observation, study, and experience. Certain children remain on the side
lines; others are always in the full swing of things. Some play in large,
noisy gangs. Little girls such as Kathy and Linda prefer less action and
more talk.

It is natural for children to use the bathroom and wash their hands
when they return to the kindergarten. A refrigerator in one corner holds
milk, and each child takes out his own carton, drinks it, puts the empty
container into a receptacle, and stretches out on the floor for a brief
rest.

Rest (10:00–10:15)

The kindergarten floor is vinyl tile and beautifully cared for. There is
no concern about drafts, for the floor is radiant heated. Mothers are
eager to send rugs for rest, but the physician says that unless these rugs
are washed daily, they have more germ-carrying potential than a clean,
warm floor.

The room is quiet, and the atmosphere is conducive to rest and relaxation. The teacher sits at the piano and offers a brief concert of soothing, gentle music. Other days, she uses a music box or a record as
background for the rest period. This is a time for repose, tranquillity,
contemplation, and those farfetched wonderful daydreams of childhood.

Group Experience—A Quiet Time to Learn Together (10:15)

The children have had their vigorous play, their midmorning snack,
rest, and relaxation. They are alert, fresh, and calm now. The appropriate activity is a lesson in literature, music, science, the presentation of a
new art form, or a discussion of work that has been going on.

Photo by RoseAnna Tendler Worth

In kindergarten, academic lessons are informal, but this does not mean that they are shallow or slipshod. During these brief lessons the scope and depth of learning depend on the teacher's skill in stimulating the child's learning processes rather than on her method of concocting an information capsule for child consumption.

Literature

Hardly a day passes in kindergarten without a story. A book must be brief, its pictures lovely, and the storyteller full of animation. Little children are susceptible to many forms of literature,[25] including stories, poetry, chants, and dramas.

Dramatization, especially, comes naturally to little children. Karen, for instance, announces one day that she would like to be Mary. Would someone be her lamb? Out of this inspiration grow other brief dramatizations, with children inventing their dialogue and pantomime. A feeling for the purity of words and sensitive role playing are part of the little child's natural endowment. Adults often exploit and contaminate this inborn gift when they drill and rehearse the little child for a "performance." This type of display is the surest way to obliterate the kindergartner's natural inspiration and to make him self-conscious and pretentious.

Not only are the experiences of hearing stories and other forms of literature important, but the joy of hearing them again and again is even more meaningful, for it gives the child a feeling that loveliness is enduring. A child's identification with characters, his interpretations and sympathy, all pave the way for his future as a reader of taste and reflection. Enjoyment of literature also inspires the child to invent his own poetry and stories, especially when the teacher and the class listen, respect, and encourage such creativity.

Music

To the kindergartner, music is a natural, spontaneous expression. He always seems to be humming a little tune or singing a song: indoors, outdoors, at work, at play. And as he sings, his body moves—to a finger play, to a march, a hop, a skip, a jump. No kindergarten teacher ever complained of having to interest her class in musical activity. All she needs is a sense of perception and the knowledge that will enable her to capture this simple joy and give the child a glimpse of the treasures of music. When the teacher is in constant touch with music, her own unquenchable zest for this experience is absorbed by the children in her presence.[26]

Even the simplest little song can be made a lesson in pitch through an awareness of the highs and lows. Dynamics comes through the softs and louds. Harmony is the blend of voices, the structure of chords, the combination of instruments in the rhythm band. The teacher's playing of a simple glissando fires the child's imagination: it could be an avalanche, an escalator, a rocket being fired, a kite snatched up by the wind! The child interprets with his imagination, dramatizes with his body, and develops a poetic ear.

Listening to music is a lifelong experience, and here, too, the teacher in her manner of presentation whets the musical appetite of the little child. The musical fare for kindergarten listeners must be superb, whether the teacher offers the musical stories of Prokofiev or the tinkling little rondos of Haydn and Mozart. This skill of exposing children to an art form grows with the teacher, and often inspires her to advance

Photo by RoseAnna Tendler Worth

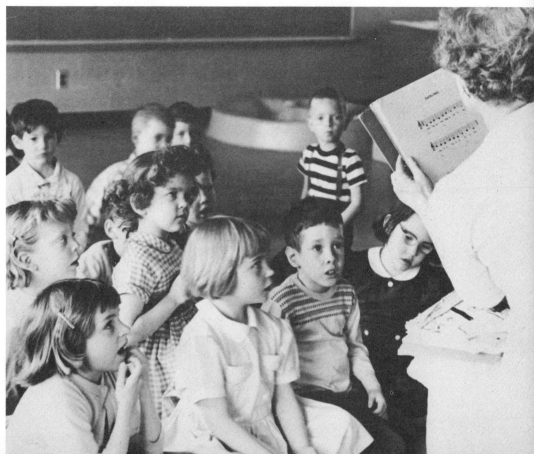

her own musical studies. As a matter of fact, many teacher-musicians choose kindergarten as a career because of the chance it gives to use music.

Again, the kindergarten child must be given a taste of creativity. John invents a simple little chant, and eagerly sings it to the other children. The glory of having his classmates admire it is great indeed. But think of how he feels when the teacher strikes his tune on the piano, his classmates sing it back, and when he returns the next day, there it is—written in the language of music, on a large poster, with the title "John's Song!" Is there any doubt that the ecstasy of recognition will nurture the process of creation?

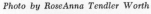

Photo by RoseAnna Tendler Worth

Science

There is so much in the physical world a child wants to know that it is difficult to plan a narrow, precise science curriculum for the kindergartner. It is best, in fact, when science lessons are provoked by a child's firsthand experience and curiosity.

When Linda asks the simple question, "What is a leaf?" she starts a chain of exploration that involves the class for days. The relationship of leaf to bud, leaf to branch, tree, roots, earth, and life itself comes in a sequence of experiments, observations, films, pictures, conversation. The child even at this tender age learns of the veins and blades of leaves, the process of photosynthesis, the effects of seasonal changes on plant life.

Incentives for kindergarten science come from the things that are closest to children.[27, 28] An anthill in the far corner of the playground, a day of rain and fog, the familiar sight of a squirrel gathering acorns, a flight of birds seen through the classroom window, a car that refuses to start, the insides of a telephone, the batteries of a flashlight, the structure of a bird's nest—all are phenomena worthy of science explorations in the kindergarten.

Science in the kindergarten, as in any other laboratory, is a combination of "doing" and theory. Jerry brings in an old, discarded alarm clock, and asks, "What makes it tick?" The first time this question is asked, the kindergarten teacher will not know the answer, but she will lose no time in finding out. She will acquaint herself with the insides of the clock, and take it apart, piece by piece, in the presence of her class. Oh, the lessons that come from a discarded alarm clock: the concepts of time, the movements of the earth, the meaning of the hours on the clock's face, and the ingenious mechanism of spring and wheel for the process of recording time.

Children also are curious about mysterious and distant phenomena. "What is it like up in the moon?" asks Jimmy, and the teacher brings in simple, comprehensive books filled with vivid illustrations of the moon's surface, along with a film. The film is geared for children of the middle grades, yet the five-year-old comprehends amazingly when the teacher is skillful at guiding the discussion and respecting the questions posed by children. What is the temperature of the moon? Where does the moon get its light? Why is its gravity weaker than the gravity of earth? How did the mountains, craters, and seas form on the moon's surface? Why does a person weigh less on the moon than on earth? This is not an armchair fantasy of a future science lesson. It is a brief sampling of the questions raised in an actual kindergarten after the viewing of a science film.

What is a science lesson in kindergarten? It is everything and anything. It is the release of energy in an alarm clock, the chemistry of breadmaking, the process of photosynthesis in the leaf, the study of amphibians through polliwogs caught in a stream, the shaking of a jar of cream to extract butter—and when that butter is spread on crackers a lesson in chemistry has a gastronomic finale. Science is learned best by little children when it comes through the experience of the senses, simple experiments, enriched materials, and exciting discussion.

Graphic and Plastic Arts

To "teach" a young child clay modeling, finger painting, or any other art expression, is a risky practice, for it interferes with the child's individual creative process. If the teacher provides a good place to work, good modeling materials, bright, well-mixed paints, large paper, and a variety of other things to work with, the child's own artistic development will emerge.[29]

Little children often like to use these materials in ways that look messy to the adult. Paste, for instance, is a tempting substance to apply with fingers. A crayon behaves differently when used sideways. The smearing of tinted liquid starch over glazed paper gives a wonderful sensation to the fingers, and produces interesting designs. These and other sensations and experience with artistic materials are the beginning of a child's artistic productivity. Next, the child will make unrecognizable objects for which he has a name. Eventually those won-

Photo by George D. Margolin

derful, delightful likenesses of houses, people, animals, trees, and flowers will emerge.

Art is a private, precious experience, and a child's individual expression in this area must be respected. During Halloween, for instance, it is one thing to make orange and black paper available. It is quite another to insist that every child produce a cat, witch, or pumpkin face. It is stifling and destructive to pass out tracing patterns of these Halloween symbols and insist that every child trace, color, and cut them.

Of course pumpkins and cats will creep into the art work around Halloween, and hearts will be evident during the valentine season because holidays are gay and contagious. But regardless of the holiday, those children who wish to continue making their special houses, airplanes, boats, smears, and scribbles, should not be forced to interrupt a labor of love in order to manufacture holiday art products.

The commercial workbooks and coloring books which strive to combine and coordinate artistic and prereading skills are often forced on the kindergarten teacher. These materials may keep children busy but they also impair the creative vitality of the child's art work and force a pseudo approach to reading which can well result in ruining the child's chances for reading success in first grade. A teacher ill prepared and ignorant of kindergarten work welcomes these materials as time fillers. But the teacher who knows the true function of kindergarten and has an understanding of the five-year-old deeply resents their presence. Too often the appealing gimmick of the textbook salesman takes precedence over the kindergarten teacher's knowledge and experience.[30] Wherever there is a systematic use of workbooks and coloring books in kindergarten, creativity, imagination, and individuality are impeded. Workbooks do have their place as companions to texts in various subject-matter areas, but they do not belong in kindergarten!

Work-Play (10:20–11:00)

Again the children scatter, as they did outdoors, but now they use the facilities available in the kindergarten room: blocks, sand, water, paint, finger paint, the doll corner, the chalk board for printing and drawing, books to look at, pets to feed, plants to water, sets of numbers and letters to use at the felt board, and many things to touch and examine.

Some children stay with one activity through most of the work-play period, but others like to sample a variety of activities. In this span of time it is not uncommon for the child to model something with clay, spend time at the bookcase, put a puzzle together, and eventually ar-

Photo by RoseAnna Tendler Worth

rive at the doll corner for a cup of tea. This is a fine time for social experiences: working with a small group at the felt board, joining the
group who are busy with scissors, crayons, and paste, walking around
the room a bit to look at the efforts of others, and eventually having
that cup of tea. The work-play time is the part of the day that kindergarten children are most reluctant to give up. Even when there is a
trip to the auditorium or a special celebration, the kindergarten child
repeats persistently, "But when do we play; when do we work?"

Cleanup (just before 11:00)

Like all wonderful times, the work-play period must come to an end each day. Materials and equipment must be put away, work aprons hung up, the doll corner tidied, the blocks stacked. When the room is arranged in a simple, orderly way, and everything has a logical place, this housekeeping chore is conducive to a growing sense of order.

Early in the school year the cleaning up takes longer and requires more teacher assistance. In time, children develop competence and responsibility as well as a feeling of pride and respect for their room and its possessions. There is no penalty for clumsy or sloppy efforts and no high praise or reward for efficiency. Extra time is usually granted to the artists who cannot bear to abandon half-finished work. Those who have had little to put away willingly help others who used the more complicated and intricate materials and equipment.

Another Quiet Time (11:00)

Now is the time to shift into low gear. It has been a busy morning. Lunch time is near. A calm period assures a peaceful departure. It is a good time for a circle game such as "Skip to My Lou," or "Rig-a-jig-jig," with only one or two children on their feet, while the rest chant the song, sitting down, drawn together by the circle. Perhaps there is time for a brief story, a special record, or a favorite song. Occasionally a child uses this time to tell what he is thinking or proudly displays something he has just made. Then the children get their wraps.

Those who are skilled with zippers, buttons, shoelaces, and buckles help the rest. No fetish is made of these skills, since a child's pride, group incentive, and his own developing ability and eagerness to grow up eventually enable him to do a competent job of dressing himself.

The morning is over—and the teacher stands at her door as the children leave for home. The farewells are affectionate. Pat waves goodby. Joan embraces the teacher and whispers in her ear, "Don't forget to show those afternoon kids the castle I made in the sandbox." John and Christopher have their arms around each other: they are going to have lunch together, and Christopher's mother is waiting in her car.

Photo by George D. Margolin

PART III. THE IMPACT OF SPACE, EQUIPMENT, AND MATERIALS

"But you, children of space, you restless in rest,
You shall not be trapped nor tamed."

THE PROPHET

Kahlil Gibran

CHAPTER 1

THE KINDERGARTEN ROOM:
SPACE TO LIVE AND LEARN

The kindergarten room is the child's home away from his family, his social hall for meeting friends, his workshop, studio, and laboratory for learning. This room must delight his senses, protect his well-being, and excite his intellect with its wonders and challenge.[31]

From the beginning of the American kindergarten movement the builders of schools visualized this as an idyllic spot. Even in some of the oldest kindergartens there is a fine feel for space, a respect for light, and an eagerness to feed the aesthetic appetites of little children.

One kindergarten of the late twenties, for instance, features a lovely window bay with a curved built-in seat where children can sit and gaze at a purple, hilly landscape below. The doors are paneled in stained glass depicting characters out of *Mother Goose*. Everywhere in the room there are unexpected nooks and crannies of enchanting detail and charm. Such an elegant kindergarten room would be prohibitive today. Furthermore, much of its embellishment and detail contradicts the underlying philosophy of contemporary school architecture. The modern school architect is far more interested in creating a room that will stimulate the child's imagination than in a permanent exhibit for adult murals, stained glass, sculpture, and other artistic creations.

81

Even a community well able to afford extravagance today prefers schoolrooms of simple, free-flowing lines, natural materials, and an absence of ostentation.

Architectural firms like Jahr-Anderson-Machida of Dearborn, Michigan, take great pains to become familiar with the needs and characteristics of child groups, and when a school-building plan is in process, the architects and designers often consult with teachers at every step. Teachers usually have a voice in the conception of the school, the blueprints, and even the last-minute changes necessary after construction is under way. An omniscient school architect, vain enough to work without the help of teachers, faces the consequence of their criticism and animosity if they have to work in a monument of his mistakes.

Photo by RoseAnna Tendler Worth

A kindergarten room must talk to children. It must be challenging and enchanting in color, shape, and layout. It must provide freedom of movement for the restless, active child and permit the solitary child to work uninterrupted. It must be conducive for small groups of children to cluster in various parts of the room, yet permit the entire class to engage in a common activity with a feeling of spaciousness.

What is good for the kindergarten room in the way of space, equipment, and materials is good for all young children, differing mainly in scale and complexity. The child who lives in an architectual Valhalla during the kindergarten year too often finds himself in a claustrophobic cubicle in the first grade. There is real harm done when he advances from the environment of natural freedom of movement to a room where the greatest part of his day is spent at a desk with his body in an ever-lasting perpendicular position. Those who study child groups and their spatial requirements agree that each child needs between forty and sixty square feet of space, and that all classrooms, regardless of age or grade, should be limited to a capacity of twenty-five.[32]

Adequate space is the most crucial feature in a classroom. Walls, floor, heat, ventilation, light, sanitary facilities, appropriate furniture, and a satisfactory area for the storage of wraps are also important to the life of a group of children.

The walls of a kindergarten room have an influence on the emotional climate in the class. A new kindergarten room is seldom built with all the walls of the same material or color. One wall may be entirely of glass, one of cork, one of cinder block or wood paneling, and one with sections of pegboard and slate, to give children a generous space to work with chalk.

The floor is a natural place for little children to work and play. Therefore, the trend is to have radiant heat in the kindergarten floor in order to prevent drafts. It is also important that the floor be of a material that will absorb noise (this goes for ceilings, too), clean easily, and wear well. Linoleum and a variety of rubber and vinyl tiles are the best popular floor surfaces for kindergartens. Such surfaces are attractive, safe, and suitable for a variety of kindergarten activities.

Heat and Ventilation. A constant room temperature between 68° and 70° is recommended for all classrooms. The thermostat in a kindergarten should be about forty-five inches from the floor in order to enable the teacher to regulate heat at the child's height. Fresh or reconditioned air should be circulated at the rate of ten to thirty cubic feet per child per minute.

Control of Light. Windows provide the most natural and direct source of light. Indirect and fluorescent light are good artificial sources, and should be placed to assure equal light in all parts of the room. Electrical outlets must also be available on the walls of the kindergarten room for the use of a record player, tape recorder, aquarium, projector, and other important pieces of educational equipment that require electrical current.

Sanitary Facilities. Every kindergarten room needs an adjoining bathroom equipped with exhaust fan and sink. The present accepted ratio is one toilet to every ten children, but kindergarten teachers feel that a ratio of one to five would be far more realistic. There are conflicting opinions as to whether the toilets should or should not have doors on them for children of this age. From my own experience, I find that the child of five, with his growing sense of propriety, often expresses the need for privacy in performing intimate bodily functions. A stall wall about four feet high offers the child privacy and still permits the teacher to see if her help is needed. The sink for hand washing, both in the bathroom and in the kindergarten room, should be large, with multiple faucets, automatic tepid water, and a disposal-type drain, since children often wash off clay, sand, paint, paste, and other materials that clog an ordinary drain. An ample supply of liquid soap and paper toweling should always be available.

Photo by George D. Margolin

Coat Area. How to build an area for storing all the children's wraps and possessions without ruining the appearance of the kindergarten room is a continuous problem. Each child needs his own compartment for his things, with a cubby above for hat and mittens, and a compartment below for boots or rubbers. The coat area should be located on the wall nearest to the heating outlet, to permit wraps to dry in wet and winter weather.

Furniture. With so much beautiful school furniture available today, schools have to exercise restraint against the temptation to overfurnish. A new kindergarten can be so cluttered with tables and chairs that the original goal of providing adequate floor space is defeated. Such cluttering sometimes occurs when the school authority in charge of

Photo by RoseAnna Tendler Worth

purchasing is better informed on the durability of furniture than on the needs of children. A school district that consults its kindergarten teachers in this matter often saves itself a lot of money.

One kindergarten benefited greatly when the elementary principal and the teacher decided to omit tables. Instead, formica work counters were constructed along the north cork wall, where children could tack up their own pictures, and along the south glass wall, where they could enjoy a lovely view as they worked. These counters and handsome stackable chairs provided a sufficient seating and work area without loss of precious floor space. The piano, a file cabinet, colorful wall cupboards, and a few sturdy cabinets for filing children's pictures were the only pieces of furniture purchased, thus diverting furniture money toward more equipment and materials.

CHAPTER 2

EQUIPMENT AND MATERIALS:
THE TOOLS FOR WORK AND PLAY

Play is the little child's most natural and enjoyable activity. It is his way of expressing himself from morning till night, a heaven-sent process for learning some of the earliest lessons in life. With increasing insight into this activity, kindergarten teachers speak more and more of a combined *work-play* time instead of designating these as separate activities in the course of the kindergarten day.

As we have noted, a child at play is really a child at work: discovering, exploring, integrating knowledge and skills. In kindergarten he does this through the structures he builds, the pictures he paints, the many roles he plays, and the needs he fills, whether they are a physical need to climb higher, an emotional need to make-believe, a growing social need for a relationship with other children, or an intellectual desire to absorb knowledge.

With the child's play activities in mind, the kindergarten teacher outlines her school year, offering increasingly complex intellectual experiences, broader contact with the arts, and guidance to help the child gear himself for the skills the culture will expect him to learn. For this goal the teacher needs perceptivity in her relationship with the child, and equipment and materials to help him advance. Since the child's

88

Photo by George D. Margolin

play exalts every facet of his being, we cannot classify the tools of his play for distinct purposes. All pieces of equipment and materials have multiple uses. They must at all times be whatever the child wants them to be.[33]

Outdoor Equipment. For a long time the outdoor play area, or "playground," was regarded as a place for limited and circumscribed activity. The children used it mainly for "recess," as a relief from the sedentary and cerebral tasks of the classroom. For this midmorning and midafternoon break the children would bring snacks to nibble and share with friends. When the children became visibly aimless or aggressive, the teacher would distract them by organizing a circle game. Most of the time, however, this outdoor period was regarded as a short breathing spell for the teacher, too, offering an opportunity for a bit of fresh air and a momentary chance to relax.

Playground areas are now used with a different purpose. We treasure them as valuable outdoor education facilities, and estimate the needs of almost 150 square feet per child. The modern kindergarten playground directly adjoins the kindergarten room, offering safety, shade, and a variety of surfaces: a hard one for riding wheel toys; grass for running, jumping, playing; soil for gardening; sand and a nearby water outlet; and various resilient materials under such permanent pieces of equipment as swings, slides, and jungle gyms where falls are apt to occur.

The outdoor playground permits much physical freedom, but it should also be equipped and arranged to encourage social relationships, the use of imagination and make-believe, and the privilege of seclusion. A listing of outdoor equipment could go on for pages. There are available on the market a variety of climbers, ladders, boards, sawhorses, snow shovels, bridges, swings, gangplanks, fiberglass play puddles, play sculptures, spiral slides, mazes, playwebs, and other pieces of outdoor gear. Some are stationary, others are movable, and especially conducive to imaginative and dramatic play as well as providing good opportunities for developing large muscles.[34]

In spite of the wonderful advances in the design and construction of outdoor play equipment, the wheel toy, which is one of the little child's most valued outdoor tools, has been ignored. Wagons, bikes, scooters, tractors, fire trucks, and other child transportation vehicles break down all too soon with heavy kindergarten use. The design and construction of heavy-duty wheel toys would fill an urgent need in outdoor kindergarten play equipment.

Indoor Equipment. Since the kindergarten child needs a broad program of education through varied experiences, the kindergarten room must provide the equipment to make those experiences possible.

Block building is one of the most engrossing activities in the kindergarten. The large hollow blocks that come in sets of eighty are hard wood, of smooth finish, and cut in squares of 11″ × 11″ × 11″, rectangles as large as 22″ × 11″ × 5½″ and 5½″ × 11″ × 5½″. They come with various accessories such as play boards, a steering wheel and block, hollow triangles, barrels, and other pieces that add interest to the play.

Along with giving a child the opportunity to build structures large enough for him to move in, these blocks make cooperation inevitable, since a child of five is rarely satisfied to use them alone. The only disadvantage of hollow blocks is that one set is hardly enough to feed the imagination and enterprise in a group. Expensive as they are, their durability and challenge are good reasons for the presence of two sets in different parts of the room.[35]

Carpentry. This activity is one that little boys, especially, find irresistible if they have enough opportunity really to work at it. There are some boys who do carpentry work daily, and most every other little boy sooner or later makes something that takes from a day to a week to complete. Three workbenches, six vises, and enough hammers, nails, saws, planes, sandpaper, brace and bits, lumber, and other accessories give little boys an opportunity to learn eye-hand coordination (you just

Photo by RoseAnna Tendler Worth

have to hit that nail on the head!), experiment in design, and learn the art of pooling skills. Girls enjoy working at this activity, too, but their endurance and interest are usually fleeting.

Active Play. The activities described in the section on outdoor play fit into this category. Children are active indoors as well, but when the outdoor play area is adequate and the time allowed is satisfying, there is less active play indoors. The most typical pieces of equipment found indoors for this purpose are a rocking boat, a climbing box, a sandbox, trays for water play, and other pieces, depending on the scale and lay-out of the room. There are many kindergartens where, thanks to the imagination of fathers and school authorities, the rooms have such de-lightful built-in features as climbing balconies, jungle gyms, and other intriguing pieces to fill the child's need for climbing, sliding, and jump-ing, especially on days when weather prohibits outdoor play.

Less active building and manipulative play is carried on alone or in small groups, on the floor, at a table, or a counter. While the child's body is comparatively quiet, his imagination and small muscles work at great speed. In these activities he may be working with smaller unit blocks, trains, boats, airplanes, rubber dolls, wooden beads, spools, pegs, nuts, bolts, puzzles. He may be playing a game of picture Lotto, manipulating a puppet family, placing pegs on a board in his own special design, or using a combination of these toys and materials to tell a story, dramatize a situation, solve a problem.

Science experiences demand not only the basic aquarium, planting boxes, pets and their appropriate cages and hutches, but such special

Photo by George D. Margolin

pieces as compasses, garden tools, magnets, magnifying glasses, a ter-
rarium, thermometers, and prisms. Food for pets, seeds and bulbs for
planting, and chemicals for experimental purposes must all be purchased at the appropriate time. A basic set of science books on the kindergarten shelf for children to look at and interpret and for the teacher
to use in reference work are also important.

Audio visual equipment and supplies not only enrich the program, but
help to provide numerous vicarious experiences for the child. Movie
and strip film projectors, a television set, and interesting exhibits should
be available to enlarge the young child's world.

Music is one of the most natural and spontaneous activities in kindergarten. It is experienced in many ways, requiring as much and varied
equipment as possible. The piano is the biggest and most expensive musical tool. A record player, rhythm instruments, music books, a growing
record collection, an auto harp, and a chromatic xylophone are all important for musical experiences.

Creative art work is carried out with the aid of basic new materials and
useful discards. Painting gives a little child the most complete satisfaction when he can work with a large brush with a long, thick handle.
Other basic art materials are clay, chalk, finger paint, paste, scissors, and
a variety of paper materials such as construction paper, glazed paper,
newspaper, and some good art paper whenever the budget permits a
splurge. Easels are recommended for kindergarten use by many kindergarten experts, but kindergarten teachers often find them more pic-
turesque than practical. A washable flat surface is satisfactory for both
child and teacher.

Housekeeping and doll play. The props to develop fantasies and a place
to act them out are the priceless privileges of childhood. At age five
much of the cultivation of make-believe revolves around the classic
kindergarten spot known as the "housekeeping corner." Here, in the

presence of child-sized household furniture, kitchen equipment, dishes, pots and pans, dolls, buggies, and other household accessories that can be used realistically, children play house with the help of a trunkful of dress-up clothes. The imaginative, therapeutic, and social values of this play have been discussed in numerous books and articles. In addition to the "housekeeping corner," some kindergartens provide a sturdy wooden play house with furniture and dolls constructed to scale. The dollhouse is an intriguing piece of equipment, and several children are usually absorbed with it, rearranging furniture, manipulating play people, and having fun.

Language Arts. Each kindergarten needs its own library, with books for the teacher to read and discuss, and for the children to handle, use

Photo by George D. Margolin

for pleasure, and wear out. When books are handled with great frequency and respect in kindergarten, children will be eager to learn reading in first grade.

THE SCHOOL BUS

Every kindergarten should have access to the school bus. Educational trips are important ways of offering the child firsthand laboratory experiences. Some teachers depend on parents to provide transportation for such occasions, but this is a tremendous responsibility and carries great safety risks. A permanent school bus with a qualified driver is needed to make possible the trips that offer children an exciting supplement to basic education.

How does the urban and suburban child learn about a fruit farm, a dairy farm, a zoo, a museum, an airport, a train station, a post office, and other wonderful places where people are working to provide the food, shelter, services, and the aesthetic functions of life? Visiting places, seeing people in the community at work, and returning to the classroom for more detailed studies of the places and people visited are a wonderful way of bringing the social studies to life. In the last twenty-five years industries, museums, stores, and social institutions have made members of their staffs with backgrounds in education available as guides to the school children who want to look and learn.

PART IV. THE INTERPLAY OF PEOPLE

"No man can reveal to you aught but that which already
lies half asleep in the dawning of your knowledge."

THE PROPHET

Kahlil Gibran

CHAPTER 1

THE TEACHER

The word *teacher* appears repeatedly in this book, for *teacher, child,*
and *learning* are an inseparable triangle. The emotional climate of the
classroom emanates from the teacher, just as the family spirit is sustained by the parents. The teacher's influence and impact on the individual child and the classroom family of children are penetrating,
enveloping, immediate, and enduring. Through the magic of the
teacher-child relationship many a rough little stone has been polished
to unbelievable brilliance. By an equally contrasting stroke, the spirit
of a most promising child has been stifled and crushed.

As his initial educator, the kindergarten teacher bestows upon the
little child the school's bounty from that first day when the neophyte
scholar stands before her—innocent, half-thrilled, half-scared, and completely awed with anticipation. From this moment she plays her double
role.

First, she is the parent away from home, and in this role her authority must be fraught with such tenderness that it melts away the
most hardened thoughts and brings the most hostile feelings under
control. Such delicacy of authority is necessary in all teachers, but the
teacher of kindergarten children must also be endowed with infinite
patience for the child's littleness, helplessness, and inexperience.

97

Second, the teacher must pave the way for learning through her faith, support, guidance, and recognition. There is no assurance that material in the teacher's plan book will reach the child just because the teacher uses it. Learning occurs only when the learner gives consent;[36] knowledge is absorbed when the relationships and the setting facilitate the process. To help the child learn, the teacher must possess two indispensable qualities: she must be first a great humanitarian and second, a dedicated learner.

What is the nature of the teacher's learning? No teacher ever stops learning about children, and the most indelible learning is in the living. Parents, too, offer the teacher an avenue of learning as well as a treasured source of growth, expansion, and friendship. The teacher learns also from her colleagues, administrators, and her community. But the most intimate and profound learning comes from her own deepening, maturing, mellowing life.

A teacher used to be forbidden marriage if she wanted a career with children. Now she teaches, marries, rears her own family, and returns again to her work, a more accomplished and richer person. Not only are teachers coming to the kindergarten from homemaking and child rearing, but also from other professions.

In the role of supervising teacher, I have had the thrill of working with many promising undergraduates, as well as with mature, post-degree students coming from such diversified careers as botany, social work, music, horticulture, geology, art, nursery school, nursing, the armed forces, and business. These women in their twenties, thirties, and forties had left their respective professions because they preferred to use their gifts in a life with young children. Some were mothers. Others, still unmarried, decided that this would be valuable experience prior to homemaking and children of their own. As our young horticulturist said, "All of my family work in our greenhouse. We love to grow healthy, beautiful plants. I feel that many of the laws of horticulture are applicable in the kindergarten." Not only was her reasoning sound, but this young teacher-scientist opened a new world of enchantment to all of us.

TRIPS AND PLANS

THREE LITTLE PIGS

Photo by George D. Margolin

Teachers, because of their past restricted life, used to grow rigid and embittered toward children. Today this is inexcusable. There are endless opportunities for advanced academic work, stimulating professional conferences, on-the-job research, travel experiences, and certainly the pursuit of one's hobbies and avocations. School systems in many parts of the country are encouraging teachers to study by helping finance university courses, conferences, and workshops. Such an investment pays a community rich dividends in the quality and character of its cultural level.

A vast difference exists between a teacher who is ever-probing, growing, exploring, learning, and one who has mastered a set of techniques for hoodwinking children into conformity and diminishing the grandeur of learning by presenting a tightly-organized, annually-repeated bag of tricks. When a teacher continues to expand as a person and a learner, the humanitarian and scholarly gifts in her children expand.

CHAPTER 2

THE KINDERGARTEN PARENT

A child sometimes lives in two separate worlds: the world of home and the world of school. And in this divided existence he encounters different styles of adult authority as well as conflicting values and expectations. In many communities, however, the dichotomy is disappearing because home and school, teacher and parent, are working together from the beginning of the child's school career. Out of this harmony the child reaps the benefits. Without it, the school and home often work at cross purposes, with the child caught in a perplexing squeeze. The continuous flow of communication between parent and teacher is one of the best safeguards against this dilemma.

During the kindergarten year there are many reasons for parent and teacher to be in close contact. The parent's participation in study groups, parent-teacher conferences, classroom projects, trips, and holiday celebrations brings the parent into the child's world in a meaningful, fascinating way. It also gives the parent a grasp of the philosophy, practices, and goals of the kindergarten experience.

Does a great amount of parent activity usurp the authority of the teacher? Does it overstimulate the group? Not if there is complete understanding that the teacher is the pro and the parent the enthusiastic, facilitating amateur. It is the teacher who assumes the respon-

Photo by George D. Margolin

sibility for child and curriculum, but the more polished a performer she is, the more skillful will be her ability to blend parent contributions into the substance of the curriculum.

Parents are sometimes reluctant to volunteer their services in kindergarten, and wait unnecessarily for an invitation from the teacher. Overemphasis on social amenities creates a needless barrier in establishing the necessary contact between home and school. From the teacher's viewpoint, it is completely appropriate for the parent to take the first step in offering services, time, and skill. The more contacts the parent has with the school, the more relaxed, spontaneous, and beneficial the relationship. There is hardly an area of work in the classroom where parents cannot enrich the experience of learning.

One mother sent her child to school with a collection of leaves from the deciduous trees of her garden, without realizing that her hobby of pressing and preserving leaves was a significant contribution to a lesson on plant life. Another mother, while in the process of planting bulbs, offered to put some into the school garden; the teacher invited her to come and do this with the children. Guppies and snails donated from a home aquarium offered a wealth of opportunity for the study of water animals. A turtle found on a country road added an interesting pet to the classroom.

Capitalizing on the curiosity of little children, a kindergarten teacher launched a study on fathers' occupations. One by one the fathers came into the kindergarten for a brief visit with the children, after making previous arrangements with the teacher. The doctor-father opened his medical bag and discussed the use of its contents. The plumber, electrician, and carpenter came with their toolboxes. Other fathers invited the class to visit them at their places of business: the bank, the supermarket, the newspaper office.

Many a parent has enriched the art activities of the kindergarten by contributing discards to the collage box. Old magazines for cutting up and pasting, colored yarn, empty spools, pieces of fabric, boxes of various shapes and sizes, ready-made starch for finger paint, sawdust, pieces of tile. Experience in putting unusual and interesting materials together in child-conceived designs is a necessary prelude to the more deliberate and disciplined artistic creation which will eventually emerge.

The kindergarten homemaking corner is a wonderful spot for parent contributions. Old hats, shoes, bags, ties, jackets, and other clothes discarded by the parents are effective and useful in the kindergarten dress-up trunk. Dough brought to school by a mother, and baked in the school kitchen, adds a delicious touch to the "tea party" play. Old baby clothes, receiving blankets, and other baby equipment are useful in playing "house." A mother coming into the kindergarten with her featherweight sewing machine, tape measure, pins, and tailoring chalk during the work-play period can offer interested little girls a fascinating activity.

Photo by George D. Margolin

Photo by George D. Margolin

Music experiences in kindergarten can be wonderfully expanded with help from parents. Records can be shared. A music box can be brought in occasionally. Old barrels, boxes, and tire tubing are fine materials for making drums. Pebbles and beans are good for the inside of child-made Indian rain rattles. A parent who plays an instrument need only render a few simple melodies to launch the children's interest in a new form of music appreciation. The parent pianist, violinist, drummer, horn player, or penny whistle blower will receive a Carnegie Hall ovation for the performance of a simple composition. The mother who has had work in creative dance and comes garbed in leotard and ballet slippers gives the children an immense experience in the blending of

music and movement, as well as a tremendous outlet for large muscle
activity.

The mother librarian is an invaluable source for helping the teacher
find new books, articles, and other materials in conjunction with her
work. Her coming in to show the children a new book or tell them a
story also meets with teacher approval and child delight.

Help for the teacher in the maintenance of equipment frees her to
do more for the children. If the children rest on rugs, a working committee of mothers taking turns laundering them on Friday and deliver-
ing them on Monday relieves the teacher of a tedious responsibility. A
mother's taking over the job of checking labels in children's wraps is
another way of contributing to kindergarten housekeeping and mini-
mizing loss of children's personal possessions. In the wintertime, when
children wear many wraps, if a few mothers arrive at dismissal time
to help with buttons, zippers, ties, and straps, the teacher will have an
opportunity to dispose of some urgent last-minute chores, such as send-
ing a note home to Mary's mother, carefully wrapping a picture for
Bobby, and giving special encouragement and a little extra affection
to Nancy who has had a rough day.

Holidays are especially festive and memorable when punctuated with
a simple party or celebration. Providing paper plates, holiday napkins,
and refreshments lends joyfulness to these occasions and helps children
develop the social graces. For mothers to come into the kindergarten
at Halloween time, on Valentine's Day, before Thanksgiving, Christ-
mas, and Easter holidays, to make cookies with children or serve a
holiday meal, is popular practice in kindergartens all over the country.
There is no reason why a little brother or sister of three or four cannot
come as a visitor when his mother is helping in a celebration. It is
totally unfair, however, to send a younger child and expect either the
teacher or kindergartner to assume responsibility for him.

As we have noted, many kindergartens have a study group for parents. At these meetings parents not only meet to learn about child development and education, but also repair wheel toys, paint furniture,

build a few extra shelves, and remodel a piece of cabinetwork or a piece of equipment. These informal opportunities for work and talk start a parent's interest in his child's schooling, and eventually involve him in greater community activities. When parents begin to participate in school affairs at the kindergarten level, they assure a better life for their children and a more enlightened community for themselves.[37]

CHAPTER 3

THE INDIVIDUAL CHILD

Five is the typical age for the child to enter kindergarten. Legally, it makes him eligible for public education in a child society, under the leadership of a qualified teacher. Chronological age is the one likeness among kindergarten children. In all other respects, they differ.[38]

Children come in all sizes. Some lose their baby teeth early, some late. There are the lithe, graceful children and the lumbering, awkward ones. The serene and joyful play and work amid the sad and explosive. Each child abounds in characteristics and behaviors that can be neither measured, weighed, nor even observed with complete accuracy. For each is a unique, precious self, unlike any other living being in the world.[39]

Some children come to school already possessing academic skills. They count well, print, paint recognizable objects, read primers, spell, and do many other things because someone has taken the trouble to make available the necessary help and materials, and to answer questions or ponder them with the child. How do these children fit with other five-year-olds who may be just as bright but arrive at school completely oblivious to the alphabet, the number system, the color wheel?

In the good kindergarten, where the class size is not overwhelming, the teacher can create a climate for learning out of an amazing pot-

Photo by George D. Margolin

pourri of children. She offers no reward for virtue and no retribution for shortcomings. The corner is not for isolation, nor are children segregated and sorted out in different parts of the room on the basis of skills and abilities. The teacher's contact with the whole group strengthens each individual child, for in our democracy we cannot nurture an educational elite, even at the kindergarten level.[40] From this early contact with school, each individual child must have an opportunity to develop himself to the fullest.

When a child comes to kindergarten he brings his entire world and an already considerable life history: family background, joys, heartaches, strivings, feelings, thoughts, behaviors, his physique, and certainly his idiosyncrasies. To know something about a child's skills and abilities is quite possible. To assume one really knows *him* is indeed presumptuous.

Within a few days after school has begun, the teacher discovers that John can print and paint well. Lewis knows how to tie his shoes. Jane works puzzles with amazing speed. Ronny has a wealth of songs in his head, and sings them all on pitch.

Then, after a few more days, children relax, and begin to reveal their exasperating and immature behaviors. The child prone to thumb-sucking brings this into view. A child who has attacked others begins flexing his muscles for combat. He who has been having toilet accidents has recurrences. Even the most formidable teacher cannot always make a child do the "right" things. For the child *is* his behavior at all times, and it is only when he is free to behave in a way that is natural to him that the teacher can really reach him.[41]

How does she help him discard the trying and destructive ways? She does this in her own way, with her special brand of behavior and humanity rather than with a specific "disciplinary" trick or technique. She puts limits on his actions for his own protection and for the good of the group, but through it all she never lets him forget that he is wonderful and worthy of her love and respect. When the teacher disciplines with an overflowing heart, the child not only grows in his own feeling of self-worth, but also becomes acceptable to other children. As one little girl said to a substitute teacher who was having a rugged time, "Jimmy really isn't bad. He just *feels* bad."

A teacher does not punish for bad behavior. It is only when she sympathizes with the feelings underlying this behavior that a child is willing to discard the tormenting acts that serve him as weapons for his personal war with the human race. Punishment is not a way of eliminating the bad in a child, but rather a method of hurting *all of him*. When he is hurt in this way, his fears often prompt him to act remorseful, but his feelings grow more hostile and vindictive than ever. Just as the bad behavior cannot be dissolved through retribution, so the good cannot be installed through reward, for like the stakes on a quiz show, the rewards would have to be continually increased in order to hold incentives for the child.

Each child needs not only the teacher, but the group as well, to help him realize himself. Of course the teacher must help the child become aware of ground rules, ethics, values, and respect for the rights of others. Like the good home, the good kindergarten does this through gentleness and fair play, with such subtlety that the casual observer can barely gather from a visit or two what is really going on.

When questioned by a group of student-teacher observers as to why she let Judy "get away" with a violent display of temper, the teacher replied, "Why did I hold her close and pet her instead of scolding? To give her support, to help her realize that even when one is bad he needs to know that someone cares for him. And did you notice how she gradually thawed out and quietly joined others at play? If you think this outburst was bad, you should have seen her a few months ago!" Thus while the outside observer saw only the violence of Judy's behavior, the teacher, having faith in the child's eventual growth, could point out progress.

The mild behavior of the kindergarten teacher during a child fracas can look quite weak to those who hold clear-cut, rigid concepts of child morality and adult authority. Some would go so far as to recommend that the teacher end this nonsense with a good spanking. But the sensitive teacher cannot bring herself to use her mature physical power on an already helpless and upset child. Instead of avenging the child attacker with a beating, she consoles the child victim with love. Thus the aggressor sees sympathy for another, a far better example of human conduct than a rap on the knuckles for himself.

A kindergarten where focus is on goodness and the method is faith causes the warring child to lay down his futile weapons and tend to his own good growth strivings. When the teacher does not heap overwhelming rewards of recognition for "being good," a child is free to concentrate on being himself rather than on spending valuable energy and effort to connive for adult favor.

In the good kindergarten milieu, the individual child benefits from the wholesome group, and the goodness of his nurture increases because the contributions of each individual child are magnified and refined in the year-long life of the kindergarten. Such were the experiences of Tim and Lucy—each with a special personal difficulty, living in a kindergarten that offered them opportunity for personal enhancement.

Tim arrived alone for his pre-kindergarten spring visit. He immediately joined the group of children playing at the sandbox, and in a matter of minutes he was staging a whirlwind temper tantrum.

Nothing could pacify him, and even when the teacher tried to cuddle him, Tim kicked and bit. Finally, he was carried out of the room. When the principal drove him home, Tim's mother explained that she had not escorted her child to school because his little sister was ill, and she was awaiting the momentary arrival of the doctor. She expressed complete surprise when told that Tim was too upset to remain for the morning.

When this was reported to the kindergarten teacher, she did not find the explanation acceptable. Experience had taught her that a child who explodes in kindergarten displays temper at home as well. She knew from this initial meeting with Tim that he would need much help and patience in September.

A few days prior to the opening of school, when the teacher was working in her room, Tim's father and mother visited her. The father had an aquarium he was not using; would the teacher like it? When the mother noticed that the ironing board in the doll corner needed a cover, she took it home and covered it. It was evident that the parents were offering gifts and services to pave the way for Tim's arrival.

The first few days of school life with Tim were surprisingly calm, and the teacher recognized that he was a child of unusual brightness. But the outbursts of temper soon reappeared. When another child crossed him, when he mislaid a personal possession, when a project in which he was involved was interrupted—he exploded.

The teacher dealt gently with Tim, who was soon a perpetual disturber of the peace. She expressed sympathy when he became upset. She consoled him at the loss of a possession, and laughed with pleasure at its recovery. Gradually Tim came to understand that the teacher was his ally, and that the children also liked and understood him. As the teacher became better acquainted with Tim, she also realized that his little sister often upset his room and personal possessions at home, and that he deeply resented this. His parents punished him for hitting his little sister, and told him that she was still a baby and could not be held responsible for her actions. As a result, at school he was so obsessed with a need for possession that he refused to share any of the materials or equipment, attacking any child who came near him.

Early in November, Tim's parents asked for a conference with the teacher. His temper tantrums at home had become increasingly violent, and they were eager to know whether the teacher had to "put up" with them at school as well. The teacher admitted that he was still explosive, but she also reported that this behavior was increasingly less violent and of shorter duration. She also described the situations which provoked them, and told the parents that she had tried to understand the causes of the behavior instead of looking for an effective form of punishment. Tim evidenced a great need for privacy when he worked, and needed complete assurance that his block-building structures, paintings, and woodwork projects would not be touched or destroyed by others. At first the children resented this attitude on Tim's part, but as they became better acquainted with him, they were increasingly able to respect his wishes. "The nicest result of all," stated the teacher, "is that Tim is beginning to invite others to join him at his work. Knowing that his privacy is protected, he is starting to make social overtures toward others."

Suddenly the mother burst into tears. "The trouble with us," she cried, "is that we have been expecting too much from him. We don't realize how annoying it must be for him always to have his room and possessions invaded by Janie. We'll have to do something about protecting his rights instead of punishing him."

Tim's parents had disciplined their child with the best of intentions, but the punishment was completely unjust. When they realized, after a discussion with the teacher, that there was a basis for Tim's irritability, they felt better able to help their child. They also admitted at this interview that they as parents had not set their son good examples by controlling their own tempers.

Only parents who felt that they could say anything about themselves without loss of esteem in the eyes of the teacher would have discussed their own behavior and its impact upon their child as frankly as did Tim's.

How does the teacher discipline? Not by putting a child off in a corner nor by depriving him of something he loves to do, but by removing the impediments that cause his behavior to take a hostile path. When a child has difficulties, it is best to talk them over with the parents. In this instance the teacher was able to help the parents. There are other instances when parental insight and understanding of the child can be of great help to the teacher. Because the conference method of reporting on a child's progress offers many opportunities for strengthening the partnership of home and school, it is rapidly becoming the preferred method of reporting a child's progress to his parents.[42, 43]

It was May, and suddenly there appeared among the children a little girl, clinging to her mother, moving painfully, step by step. She was tiny, dainty, coiffured in two pigtails with ribbons on the ends.

This was Lucy's spring visit to kindergarten. Her mother had courageously brought her, on the gamble that the school might possibly allow her among normal children. It was evident to the teacher at first glance that this child was a victim of cerebral palsy.

When their eyes met, the mother said to the teacher, "She's a very sweet child, and our doctor tells us that she is bright. He recommended that we try to put her into a kindergarten with normal children, but he warned us that few teachers would be willing to take her. Is there the slightest chance . . ."

The teacher was embarrassed. She had never worked with such a child. She felt a sense of dread and apprehension, trying to visualize what life would be like if she admitted Lucy into her kindergarten.

As the teacher stood there, trying to cope with her own mixed feelings, the child suddenly reached out, grabbed her hand, and embraced her lovingly.

The mother pleaded, "You don't know what this means to her; you can't possibly imagine. I'll do anything you ask if you'll only give her a chance."

Thus, after a special arrangement was worked out between the home and school, Lucy entered kindergarten the following September. But her mother came, too. At first she stayed with Lucy through the entire morning. Then, as Lucy became more self-sufficient, the mother came only to help during special times of the morning.

During the work-play period, especially, Lucy needed the help of her mother. It was through this assistance that Lucy learned to replace the brushes she painted with in their special jars, to fit pieces of a puzzle together, to use scissors, to build with blocks, and to put away her toys. Like many handicapped children, Lucy needed more time, and knowing that this need was being met by her mother, the teacher could keep the rest of the children at their natural pace.

What of the other children in the kindergarten? They could see that Lucy was different, that her arms and legs lacked steadiness, that speech was a painful process, but they also could see the wonderful teamwork of mother and teacher in her behalf. With their inborn goodness, the children protected her from danger, helped her out of trouble, and took her graciously into their play. It was apparent that Lucy could not participate as a contributing member in all activities, but because the teacher refused to permit Lucy's handicap to keep the child from play, the children likewise developed a sense of attachment and responsibility toward Lucy.

Is this a farfetched example of integrating a handicapped child? Certainly not.[44, 45, 46] A handicapped child excluded from childhood's midst remains on the fringe of society as an adult. Children with various handicaps attend kindergarten groups: the child with the hearing aid, the blind child with an adult at his side, the spastic child—I have seen one trying to march with the group as he leaned on the arm of an ortho-

pedist—the child with the brace, and the child with the crutch. Most of
these children attend kindergarten part of the time and special classes
during the greatest part of the week, with specially qualified teachers.
Yet all of these children are thrilled beyond description in the presence
of normal children. Does the handicapped child in a kindergarten im-
pede the group? The effect of such contact is usually a twofold blessing.

By living with a handicapped child in their midst, the children of a
kindergarten develop amazing tenderness, sympathy, and responsibility.
Their fraternity and intimacy with a less fortunate child make the
kindergarten experience deeper and broader. The handicapped child,
strengthened by his contact with the group, gathers courage to take on
more challenging tasks, to feel less apart, and to reach out to life instead of withdrawing from it.

CHAPTER 4

THE EMERGING RELATIONSHIPS OF CHILDREN

The strength of a family grows out of the harmony and cooperation of its members. In the classroom this must happen on a larger, more complex scale.[11] When a child feels the brothers and sisters in his family are not dependable friends, he is unrelated and impoverished. In the classroom this circumstance is also tragic, for a child who is convinced that his classmates do not like him is neither interested in coming to school nor comfortable after he gets there.

The teacher, like the good parent, must be willing to permit emotional explosions among children whenever the need arises, for the development of good human relations does not come about when only the expressions of sweetness and light rise to the surface. Squabbles—over possessions, personal rights, and differing points of view—make up the substance and realities of life in the group. Out of these conflicts often come valuable social lessons of sharing, fair play, responsibility, and cooperation. How is such a relationship cultivated among five-year-olds?

It is accomplished through the leadership of the teacher, when she conveys to each child the feeling that she is *on his side,* and offers him opportunities to make friends. This relationship can be cultivated only when children are free to move about the classroom and playground spontaneously, to make choices, to work and play with various com-

Photo by George D. Margolin

panions, and to make mistakes. When children mingle freely, their actions often become complicated through personal conflicts, appearing, at times, hopelessly snarled. These are the crises that the support and guidance of the teacher can turn into lessons in social relationships.

In Dan's kindergarten, the block corner holds a tremendous lure, especially for little boys. In this spot one is sometimes architect, engineer, mechanic, helper, and many other characters, depending on the project of the moment. Thus the block corner is not only a kindergarten nerve center, but also a valuable avenue for social and intellectual expansion.

When a structure is erected by a group of children, a job is rarely completed without conflicts that result in eventual agreements and productivity. Thus there is more to a finished block structure than meets the eye. It is often a culmination of differing plans, ideas, and personalities fused through teamwork. It represents an expression of different children, building here day after day, free to work together, at a task of their choice. They know one another better each day, and through this familiarity and continuity they work increasingly better.

Then along comes Dan. He has been longing for weeks to join this group, and has been slowly gathering the courage to approach it. Being a naturally timid child, he had hoped in his secret fantasies that they would welcome him with open arms at the first advance, and save him the effort of seeking admittance.

But the other four do not take this viewpoint. They enjoy such an overwhelming sense of priority in this spot, with these blocks, that they refuse to include him. In fact, he eventually becomes such a nuisance that they find his presence intolerable, and throw him out bodily.

Photo by George D. Margolin

But Dan wants in.

He needs help from the teacher, who is busy with a tearful little girl. Dan's despair gradually turns to anger, and with one wrathful kick he destroys the building the other little boys have erected.

The four boys are equally angry, and they go to the teacher in a body. They make her listen. They want something done about this intruder, this terrible boy who has ruined their work, this horrible Dan.

Dan has retreated, to sulk in a secluded corner.

The teacher and the four righteous block builders seek him out. The teacher asks quietly whether he really knocked over their building, and Dan shouts, "Yes, because they wouldn't let me play." He also claims that he has as much right to the blocks as they have.

The four do not want him. A new member at this point would upset the harmony of their group. A fifth wheel is never a welcome addition. Anyhow, they announce to the teacher, Dan can't build and would only spoil their work.

Dan defends his rights. "Those blocks are for everybody, and you guys *have to* let me in."

The foursome remains firm in its refusal.

Then, John's sense of justice is suddenly touched off. "That's right," he agrees. "They are for everyone. Dan should have a turn, too."

"But he'll spoil it," cries another.

Dan pleads. "I promise not to spoil anything." Thus the clique of four becomes the gang of five.

When the dispute was brought to her attention, the teacher could have told the four boys that they had been hoarding the blocks long enough, and deprived them of their beloved corner. Or she could have favored them and punished Dan for destroying their structure. But the teacher refused to play this judgmental role. She merely stood there, listening to each side, as the little boys argued. It was during this conflict that John began to put himself in Dan's place. Through his deep sense of empathy he was able to help the group arrive at a fair and friendly solution.

If the teacher had merely taken a surface look at Dan's act, she would have seen only the ruined block structure, and felt justified in isolating him. After all, he did look like the aggressor, destroyer, and scrapper. But when the teacher *believes* in children, she does not hasten to make such short work of administering justice.

How are the crucial skills of living harmoniously with others developed in kindergarten? They are cultivated through a deep respect for the child. The kindergartner, experiencing his first taste of school, must take more than his bodily safety for granted. He must feel that this is a safe place to think his thoughts and speak his mind, even when his feelings and expressions differ markedly from the rest of the group.

Thus, a child's education journey starts in kindergarten, at age five. This is his debut, his initiation into the great, wonderful world of school. It must offer him true joy and satisfaction. It must give him a glimpse of his potential. It must convince him that a life of learning is fine and worth while. Some learning will be easy and natural. Yet, even at age five, there are moments of exasperation and anguish, of trying to "find out," of having to take pains, of learning through one's mistakes, of having to try a variety of plans for the solution of a problem. No learner can escape the frustrations of learning. That is why the little child, from the very beginning of school, must have a wonderful start.

His parents must be deeply concerned about this first year. They must be well aware of what is appropriate and good in the way of a kindergarten experience. They must be eager to support the strengths of their school, and work for the elimination of its weaknesses. When parents in a community feel this way, the teacher brings her own reverence for life and learning into view, hoping to strike, kindle, and deepen the passion for learning in each child.

How does the teacher know what knowledge a child gleans in the course of a morning in kindergarten, or how he will absorb and mobilize his growing impressions, perceptions, and discoveries? Some children tell with their shining eyes; some express themselves with an outpouring of words. There are also children such as Michael, who seem to be a

million miles away, and yet whose apparent inattentiveness is deceiv-
ing. Such children have a way of detaching a tiny modicum of knowledge, and adding it to their limitless imagination where, like a kite, it
goes over the treetops and into the clouds.

Photo by RoseAnna Tendler Worth

NOTES AND FURTHER READING

1. Parke, Mary B. *Parents and Children.* New York State *Education.* Vol. XLIII, pp. 629–30, June, 1956.
2. Donley, Marshall O. Jr. "Welcome to Our School," *NEA Journal,* Vol. 48, pp. 23–25, February, 1959.
3. Hassel, Carl. "Pre-Kindergarten Workshop," *The School Executive,* Vol. 76, pp. 56–57, June, 1957.
4. Headley, Neith. "Good Education for Five-Year-Olds," *Childhood Education,* Vol. 30, pp. 314–16, March, 1954.
5. Barclay, Dorothy. "Looking Ahead to Kindergarten," *The New York Times Magazine,* p. 35, July 29, 1956.
6. Heinz, Mamie W. "What Are the Greatest Needs of Children?" *Childhood Education.* Vol. 30, p. 351, April, 1954.
7. Montague, Patsy. "Now You Take 25 Children," *Childhood Education,* Vol. 31, No. 8, pp. 371–74, April, 1955.
8. Maul, Ray C. "Is Class Size a Factor in Recruiting Teachers?" *NEA Journal,* Vol. 45, pp. 416–17, October, 1956.
9. McConkie, Gwen W. and Hughs, Marie M. "Quality of Classroom Living Related to Size of Kindergarten Group," *Childhood Education,* Vol. 32, No. 9, pp. 428–32, May, 1956.
10. Mackintosh, Helen K. "Schools for Growing Children," *Childhood Education,* Vol. 30, pp. 304–08, March, 1954.
11. Bovard, E. W. "The Psychology of Classroom Interaction," *Journal of Educational Research,* Vol. 45, pp. 215–24, November, 1951.
12. Jenkins, David H. "Interdependence in the Classroom," *Journal of Educational Research,* Vol. 45, pp. 137–44, October, 1951.

13. Maas, Henry S. "Applying Group Therapy to Classroom Practice," *Mental Hygiene*, Vol. 35, pp. 250–59, April, 1951.

14. Stendler, Celia Burns, and Young, Norman. "The Impact of Beginning First Grade upon Socialization as Reported by Mothers," *Child Development*, Vol. 21, pp. 241–50, December, 1950.

15. Goodlad, John I. "Room to Live and Learn," *Childhood Education*. Vol. 30, pp. 355–61, April, 1954.

16. Thelen, Herbert A., et al. "Experimental Research Toward a Theory of Instruction," *Journal of Educational Research*, Vol. 45, pp. 89–93, October, 1951.

17. Nedelski, Ruth. "The Teacher's Role in the Peer Group During Middle Childhood," *Elementary School Journal*, Vol. 52, pp. 325–34, February, 1952.

18. Gladstone, R. "Do Maladjusted Teachers Cause Maladjustment?" *Journal of Exceptional Children*, Vol. 15, pp. 65–70, December, 1948.

19. Pope, Loren B. "Proposed School Aid Measure Would Delay Impact on Federal Budget," *The New York Sunday Times*, p. 13 E, January 18, 1959.

20. School District of Ferndale. *Teacher-Child Ratio at the Kindergarten Level*. Bulletin No. 1, spring, 1955. Board of Education, Ferndale, Michigan.

21. De Lourdes, Sister Mary. "The Five-Year-Old Comes to School," *National Catholic Education Association Bulletin*, Vol. 52, pp. 387–92, August, 1955.

22. Niblett, W. R. *Education the Lost Dimension*. William Sloane Associates, New York, 1955.

23. Foster, Josephine, and Headley, Neith E. *Education in the Kindergarten*. American Book Company, New York, 1948.

24. Wills, Clarice Dechant and Stagman, William H. *Living in the Kindergarten*. Follet Publishing, Chicago, 1954.

25. Arbuthnot, May Hill. *Children and Books*, Scott, Foresman and Company, Chicago, 1947.

26. Sheehy, Emma D. *There's Music in Children*. Holt, New York, 1947.

27. Zim, Herbert S. *Science for Children and Teachers*, Association for Childhood Education International, Washington, D. C., 1953.

28. Capper, Antoinette. "Small Beginnings for Four- and Five-Year-Olds." *Childhood Education*. Vol. 35, pp. 172–76, December, 1958.

29. Lowenfeld, Viktor. *Creative and Mental Growth*. Macmillan, New York, 1952.

30. Lowenfeld, Viktor. "Current Research on Creativity," *NEA Journal*, Vol. 47, pp. 538–45, November, 1958.

31. McQuade, Walter, Ed. *Schoolhouse*. Simon and Schuster, New York, 1959.

32. Laton, Donald A. "Group Processes: Some Implications in the Field of Education," *Education*, Vol. 73, pp. 135–40, October, 1952.

33. Moustakas, Clark E. *Children in Play Therapy*. McGraw-Hill, New York, 1953.

34. *Equipment and Supplies*. Association for Childhood Education International. Washington, D. C., 1957.

35. Barclay, Dorothy. "Building Character with Blocks," *The New York Times Magazine*, p. 56, March 9, 1958.

36. Rasey, Marie I., and Menge, J. W. *What We Learn from Children.* Harper and Brothers, New York, 1956.
37. *Parents and Schools, Thirty-Sixth Yearbook. The National Elementary Principal,* National Education Association, Washington, D. C., September, 1957.
38. Olson, Willard C. *Child Development.* D. C. Heath and Company, Boston, 1949.
39. Moustakas, Clark E. *The Self.* Harper and Brothers, New York, 1956.
40. Fine, Benjamin. "President's Committee Takes First Step in Plans for Expansion of Colleges," *New York Sunday Times,* p. 9 E, November 25, 1956.
41. Moustakas, Clark E. *The Teacher and the Child.* McGraw-Hill, New York, 1956.
42. Vandivar, Willis. "Preparing Parents for the Conference," *The National Elementary Principal, Thirty-Sixth Yearbook,* National Education Association, Washington, D. C., pp. 217–20, September, 1957.
43. Street, Scott W. "How Far Can Parents Go?" p. 11–20, *The National Elementary Principal, Thirty-Sixth Yearbook,* National Education Association, Washington, D. C., September, 1957.
44. Benson, Robert M. "The Hard-of-Hearing," *NEA Journal,* Vol. 47, pp. 612–13, December, 1958.
45. Galisdorfer, Lorraine. "The Partially Seeing," *NEA Journal,* Vol. 47, December, 1958.
46. Mullen, Frances A. "The Crippled," *NEA Journal,* Vol. 47, pp. 616–17, December, 1958.
47. Peckenpaugh, Adah, "The Teacher and Preventive Discipline," *NEA Journal,* Vol. 47, September, 1958, p. 372.